THE AGE OF GENIUS

1300 to 1800

MICHAEL J. BRADLEY, PH.D.

CHELSEA HOUSE
PUBLISHERS
An imprint of Infobase Publishing

The Age of Genius: 1300 to 1800

Chelsea House
An imprint of Infobase Publishing
132 West 31st Street
New York NY 10001

ISBN-13: 978-0-8160-5424-4

Library of Congress Cataloging-in-Publication Data

Bradley, Michael J. (Michael John), 1956–
    The age of genius : 1300 to 1800 / Michael J. Bradley.
        p. cm.—(Pioneers in mathematics)
    Includes bibliographical references and index.
    ISBN 0-8160-5424-X
    1. Mathematicians—Biography. 2. Mathematics, Medieval. I. Title.
    QA28.B728 2006
    510.92'2—dc22   2005032354

Chelsea House books are available at special discounts when purchased in bulk quantities for businesses, associations, institutions, or sales promotions. Please call our Special Sales Department in New York at (212) 967-8800 or (800) 322-8755.

You can find Chelsea House on the World Wide Web at
http://www.chelseahouse.com

Text design by Mary Susan Ryan-Flynn
Cover design by Dorothy Preston
Illustrations by Dale Williams

Printed in the United States of America

IBT FOF 10 9 8 7 6 5 4 3 2

This book is printed on acid-free paper.

CONTENTS

CHAPTER 6
Sir Isaac Newton (1642–1727): Calculus, Optics, and Gravity   71

CHAPTER 7
Gottfried Leibniz (1646–1716): Coinventor of Calculus   89

CHAPTER 8
Leonhard Euler (1707–1783): Leading Mathematician of the 18th Century   103

PREFACE

Mathematics is a human endeavor. Behind its numbers, equations, formulas, and theorems are the stories of the people who expanded the frontiers of humanity's mathematical knowledge. Some were child prodigies while others developed their aptitudes for mathematics later in life. They were rich and poor, male and female, well educated and self-taught. They worked as professors, clerks, farmers, engineers, astronomers, nurses, and philosophers. The diversity of their backgrounds testifies that mathematical talent is independent of nationality, ethnicity, religion, class, gender, or disability.

Pioneers in Mathematics is a five-volume set that profiles the lives of 50 individuals, each of whom played a role in the development and the advancement of mathematics. The overall profiles do not represent the 50 most notable mathematicians; rather, they are a collection of individuals whose life stories and significant contributions to mathematics will interest and inform middle school and high school students. Collectively, they represent the diverse talents of the millions of people, both anonymous and well known, who developed new techniques, discovered innovative ideas, and extended known mathematical theories while facing challenges and overcoming obstacles.

Each book in the set presents the lives and accomplishments of 10 mathematicians who lived during an historical period. *The Birth of Mathematics* profiles individuals from ancient Greece, India, Arabia, and medieval Italy who lived from 700 B.C.E. to 1300 C.E. *The Age of Genius* features mathematicians from Iran, France, England, Germany, Switzerland, and America who lived between

the 14th and 18th centuries. *The Foundations of Mathematics* presents
19th-century mathematicians from various European countries.
Modern Mathematics and *Mathematics Frontiers* profile a variety of
international mathematicians who worked in the early 20th and the
late 20th century, respectively.

The 50 chapters of Pioneers in Mathematics tell pieces of the
story of humankind's attempt to understand the world in terms of
numbers, patterns, and equations. Some of the individuals profiled
contributed innovative ideas that gave birth to new branches of
mathematics. Others solved problems that had puzzled mathematicians for centuries. Some wrote books that influenced the teaching
of mathematics for hundreds of years. Still others were among the
first of their race, gender, or nationality to achieve recognition for
their mathematical accomplishments. Each one was an innovator
who broke new ground and enabled their successors to progress
even further.

From the introduction of the base-10 number system to the
development of logarithms, calculus, and computers, most significant ideas in mathematics developed gradually, with countless individuals making important contributions. Many mathematical ideas
developed independently in different civilizations separated by
geography and time. Within the same civilization, the name of the
scholar who developed a particular innovation often became lost as
his or her idea was incorporated into the writings of a later mathematician. For these reasons, it is not always possible to identify
accurately any one individual as the first person to have discovered
a particular theorem or to have introduced a certain idea. But then
mathematics was not created by one person or for one person; it is
a human endeavor.

ACKNOWLEDGMENTS

An author does not write in isolation. I owe a debt of thanks to so many people who helped in a myriad of ways during the creation of this work:

To Jim Tanton, who introduced me to this fascinating project.

To Jodie Rhodes, my agent, who put me in touch with Facts On File and handled the contractual paperwork.

To Frank K. Darmstadt, my editor, who kept me on track throughout the course of this project.

To Karen Harrington, who thoroughly researched the material for the chapter on Pierre de Fermat.

To Warren Kay and Charles Kay, who generously allowed me to use a photograph of their collection of slide rules, and to Kevin Salemme, who took the photograph.

To Larry Gillooly, George Heffernan, Sylvie Pressman, Suzanne Scholz, and Ernie Montella, who all assisted with the translations of Latin, Italian, French, and German titles.

To Steve Scherwatzky, who helped me to become a better writer by critiquing early drafts of many chapters.

To Melissa Cullen-DuPont, who provided valuable assistance with the artwork.

To Amy L. Conver, for her copyediting.

To my wife, Arleen, who provided constant love and support.

To many relatives, colleagues, students, and friends, who inquired and really cared about my progress on this project.

To Joyce Sullivan, Donna Katzman, and their students at Sacred Heart School in Lawrence, Massachusetts, who created poster presentations for a math fair based on some of these chapters.

To the faculty and administration of Merrimack College, who created the Faculty Sabbatical Program and the Faculty Development Grant Program, both of which provided me with time to read and write.

INTRODUCTION

The Age of Genius, the second volume of the Pioneers in Mathematics set, profiles the lives of 10 mathematicians who lived between 1300 and 1800 C.E. These five centuries witnessed the end of a culturally rich period of mathematical and scientific innovation in China, India, and the Arabic countries and a renewal of intellectual life throughout Europe and the Western Hemisphere. Although mathematical innovation had stagnated in Europe after the fall of the Roman Empire, scholars in southern Asia and the Middle East preserved the mathematical writings of the Greeks and contributed new techniques to arithmetic, algebra, geometry, and trigonometry as well as the related sciences of astronomy and physics. The work of the 14th-century Iranian mathematician Ghiyāth al-Dīn Jamshīd Mas'ūd al-Kāshī typified the contributions made by hundreds of scholars during this period. He developed improved methods for approximating numerical values and introduced geometrical methods for determining areas and volumes of architectural domes, arches, and vaults.

As Europe reawakened in the early Renaissance, scholars renewed their interest in mathematics. They restored the works of the classical Greek mathematicians and familiarized themselves with advanced ideas that had been introduced in Asia and the Middle East. Universities, libraries, and scientific academies dedicated to the preservation and advancement of knowledge grew throughout Europe, gradually replacing the educational centers affiliated with royal courts and religious monasteries.

In this transitional period, amateur mathematicians—ambitious scholars who were able to supplement their limited knowledge of mathematics by teaching themselves the necessary advanced methods—played significant roles in the development of mathematics. The 16th-century French attorney François Viète revolutionized algebra by introducing a system of notation using vowels to represent variables and consonants to signify coefficients. This symbolic notation enabled him to develop general methods for solving large classes of equations and led to the development of modern algebraic notation. In the early 17th century, Scottish nobleman John Napier developed a system of logarithms that simplified the process of computation. Pierre de Fermat, another French attorney, investigated properties of prime numbers, divisibility, and powers of integers establishing the discipline of modern number theory. Frenchman Blaise Pascal, who did not attend any institutions of higher learning, invented a calculating machine, analyzed the arithmetic triangle that bears his name, and developed methods for finding areas under curves. Fermat's and Pascal's correspondence with each other about the mathematical principles involved in games of chance established the foundations of probability theory.

By the mid-17th century, an international mathematical community had developed in Europe. Scholars from many countries who were working on the same problems shared their results and their difficulties. Many mathematicians developed isolated techniques enabling them to find equations of tangent lines, locations of maxima and minima, areas under curves, and centers of mass for specific situations involving limited classes of functions. Sir Isaac Newton in England and Gottfried Leibniz in Germany synthesized their many ideas and independently developed a unified theory of calculus that impacted the development of mathematics and the methods of scientific investigation.

In the 18th century, mathematicians formalized the theoretical basis of calculus and expanded its techniques. Swiss mathematician Leonhard Euler was one of many mathematicians who contributed to the development of algebra, geometry, calculus, and number theory and applied the techniques of those disciplines to make important discoveries in mechanics, astronomy, and optics. Italian linguist Maria Agnesi used her ability to read seven languages to write a textbook that helped to unify the theory of calculus by incorporating the work of mathematicians from across the continent.

Although few scientific advances were being made in the Western Hemisphere, amateur scientists engaged in the pursuit of knowledge. Without institutions of higher learning and a network of scholars, they read, experimented, and corresponded with their European colleagues. Benjamin Banneker, a self-taught African-American tobacco farmer, typified their ambition helping to survey the boundaries of the District of Columbia and calculating the astronomical and tidal data for 12 almanacs.

Between 1300 and 1800 c.e., mathematics in Europe grew from a dormant inheritance left by Greek scholars to an active discipline in which professional and amateur mathematicians participated. The 10 individuals profiled in this volume represent the thousands of scholars who made modest and momentous mathematical discoveries that advanced the world's knowledge. The stories of their achievements provide a glimpse into the lives and the minds of some of the pioneers who discovered mathematics.

Ghiyāth al-Dīn Jamshīd Mas'ūd al-Kāshī

1

(ca. 1380–1429)

Jamshīd al-Kāshī developed methods for determining the areas and volumes of arches, domes, and vaults that are commonly used in Iranian architecture as depicted in this mosque at Samarkand. *(Library of Congress)*

Accurate Decimal Approximations

While improving on the techniques of earlier astronomers, inventing new astronomical instruments, and helping to establish the Samarkand Observatory, Jamshīd al-Kāshī (pronounced al-KAH-shee) developed innovative approximation techniques in mathematics. Using polygons with more than 800,000,000 sides and an efficient algorithm for estimating square roots, he accurately determined the value of π (pi) to 16 decimal places. He developed five methods for estimating areas and volumes of architectural arches, domes, and vaults. His iterative algorithm for approximating roots of cubic equations enabled him to determine sin(1°) to 18 decimal places. His methods of calculating with base-10 fractions completed the development of the Hindu-Arabic number system.

As the last part of his name indicates, Ghiyāth al-Dīn Jamshīd Mas'ūd al-Kāshī was born in Kāshān, Iran. The first part of his name, Ghiyāth al-Dīn, meaning "the help of the faith," was a title that a sultan gave to him later in life in honor of his scientific contributions. The brief biographical comments that he included in the introductions to some of his books and a collection of letters that he wrote to his father revealed the few known details of his life. These sources indicated that he was born about 1380 and lived most of his life in poverty. He did not disclose when or where he obtained his education, but by the beginning of the 15th century, he had focused his attention on investigations in astronomy and mathematics. The earliest event in his life that can be definitively dated was the June 2, 1406, lunar eclipse that he observed in Kāshān.

Early Astronomical Writings

Between 1406 and 1416, al-Kāshī wrote five books on various aspects of astronomy. He dedicated four of these works to the wealthy patrons who sponsored his research and writing. He carefully documented the completion of each work, often recording the month and day that he finished it. These works demonstrated his knowledge of the discoveries, theories, and methods of his predecessors; his familiarity with astronomical instruments; and his proficiency in making astronomical calculations. Collectively these books established his reputation as one of the leading astronomers of his day.

His first book on astronomy was titled *Sullam al-samā' fī hall ishkāl waqa'a li'l-muqaddimīn fī'l-ab'ād wa'l-ajrām* (The stairway of heaven, on resolution of difficulties met by predecessors in the determination of distances and sizes). Al-Kāshī completed this work in Kāshān on March 1, 1407, and dedicated it to vizier Kamāl al-Dīn Mahmūd, a high-ranking governmental official. As the title indicated, this work gave estimates for the sizes of the Sun, the Moon, and the planets as well as approximations for their distances from the Earth. The new methods he used to obtain these estimates resulted in improvements over the values that earlier astronomers had obtained. Libraries in London, Oxford, and Istanbul have preserved Arabic manuscripts of this work.

In 1410–11, al-Kāshī wrote a second book on astronomy titled *Mukhtasar dar 'ilm-i hay'at* (Compendium on the science of astronomy) that scribes later reproduced under the title *Risāla dar hay'at* (Treatise on astronomy). He dedicated this book to Sultan Iskandar, a member of the Tīmūrid dynasty who ruled Fars and Isfahān until 1414. The work presented a collection of the most frequently used theories and techniques of astronomy.

Al-Kāshī's most significant astronomical work was the *Zīj-i Khaqāni fī takmīl Zīj-i Īlkhānī* (Khaqāni astronomical tables—Perfection of Īlkhānī astronomical tables). He completed this work in 1413–14 and dedicated it to sultan Ulugh Bēg, the prince of Transoxiana (modern Uzbekistan) and son of Shāh Rukh. As the title indicated, this work was a revision of the astronomical tables produced in the 13th century by Nasīr al-Dīn al-Tūsī. The book included sections on the history of calendars, mathematics, spherical astronomy, and geometry. The lengthy introduction provided a detailed description of a method for determining the orbit of the Moon around the Earth. Al-Kāshī based this method on his observations of three lunar eclipses and on three similar observations that the second-century Greek astronomer Claudius Ptolemy had described in his classic treatise *Almagest*. The next section of the book compared six calendar systems that were currently in use throughout the world: the *Hijra*, a Muslim lunar calendar; the *Yazdegerd*, a Persian solar calendar; the *Seleucid*, a solar calendar used in Greece and Syria; the *Malikī*, a Muslim calendar developed by Omar Khayyám; the *Uigur*, a Chinese calendar; and the calendar of the Il-Khan Empire. A mathematical section provided tables of sines and tangents for angles from 0° to 180° in increments of one minute (1/60th of a degree). These tables specified each value to four sexagesimal (base-60) digits, the standard astronomical system of notation in which a number of the form 0: *a*, *b*, *c*, *d* represented

the fractional value $\dfrac{a}{60} + \dfrac{b}{60^2} + \dfrac{c}{60^3} + \dfrac{d}{60^4}$. The section on spherical astronomy included a collection of tables that accurately allowed astronomers to track the locations of the Sun, the Moon, the planets, and the stars within the universe, which was understood to be a large sphere. One set of tables provided the means to convert from ecliptic coordinates of the celestial sphere to coordinates measured from the Earth's equator, while other tables gave the longitudinal motion of the Sun, the latitudinal motion of the Moon and the planets, predictions of parallaxes and eclipses, and schedules for the phases of the Moon. A geographical section listed the latitudes and longitudes of 516 cities, mountains, rivers, and seas. The final section of the book included tables cataloging the locations and magnitudes of the 84 brightest fixed stars, listing the distances of each planet from the center of the Earth, and providing information for astrologers.

In January 1416, al-Kāshī completed a short work on astronomical instruments dedicated to Sultan Iskandar of the Turkoman dynasty, a different ruler than the one of the same name to whom he had dedicated an earlier work. In this treatise titled *Risāla dar sharh-i ālāt-i rasd* (Treatise on the explanation of observational instruments), he described the construction of eight astronomical instruments. The most well known of these was the armillary sphere, a sophisticated three-dimensional model of the universe with movable and stationary rings to represent the orbits of the planets and the locations of the stars. He also described the Fakhrī sextant, a large, fixed instrument consisting of a sixth of a circular arc that was used to determine the angle between the horizon and a star. The other instruments included the triquetrum, the equinoctial

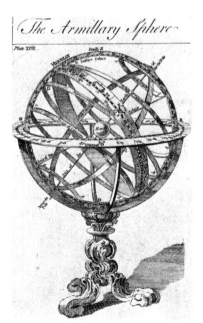

Al-Kāshī explained how to use many astronomical instruments, including the armillary sphere that represented the orbits of planets and other heavenly bodies. (*Library of Congress*)

ring, the double ring, and several variations of the armillary sphere.

On February 10, 1416, al-Kāshī finished his fifth astronomical work, *Nuzha al-hadāiq fī kayfiyya san'a al-āla al-musammā bi tabaq al-manātiq* (The garden excursion, on the method of construction of the instrument called plate of heavens). This brief book described the plate of heavens and the plate of conjunctions, two astronomical instruments that he invented. The plate of heavens was an instrument resembling an astrolabe that could be used to take measurements of the location of a planet and convert this information into a graphical format so the motion of the planet could be analyzed. The plate of conjunctions was a simpler device used to perform a type of estimation known as linear interpolation. Al-Kāshī provided additional information about these two instruments in his *Ilkahāt an-Nuzha* (Supplement to the excursion) that he wrote 10 years later.

Determining the Value of π

Between 1417 and 1424, Prince Ulugh Bēg founded a madrassa (university for the study of theology and science) and an observatory that established Samarkand as the leading intellectual and scientific center of the region. Al-Kāshī served on the university's faculty and helped to organize and equip the observatory with precision instruments, including a 100-foot-high Fakhrī sextant made of stone. In a letter to his father, al-Kāshī described Bēg as a capable scientist who led discussions, participated in critical reviews, and fully engaged in the work undertaken by the observatory's staff of 60 astronomers. In one of the prince's writings about the work conducted at the observatory, he revealed that he had a similarly high regard for his leading astronomer, singling out al-Kāshī as a remarkable scientist whose knowledge and skill enabled him to solve the most difficult problems.

One of al-Kāshī's first research projects at the observatory was to calculate the value of π with enough accuracy so that he could determine the circumference of the universe to within the thickness of a horse's hair. In *Risāla al-muhītīyya* (Treatise on the circumference), which he completed in July 1424, he provided a detailed description of the process he developed to make his precise estimate. Assuming that the universe was a sphere whose radius was no more than 600,000 times the radius of the Earth, he determined that the desired degree of precision required him to find the ratio of the circumference of a circle to its radius, $\frac{C}{r} = 2\pi$, with 16 decimal places of accuracy.

Al-Kāshī modified the geometrical technique that Greek mathematician Archimedes had used in the third century B.C.E. when he obtained the estimate $3\frac{10}{71} < \pi < 3\frac{10}{70}$. Archimedes had calculated the perimeters of regular polygons with six, 12, 24, 48, and 96 sides that were inscribed in and circumscribed about a circle. Al-Kāshī extended this process of doubling the number of sides to 28 steps, producing inscribed and circumscribed polygons having $3 \cdot 2^{28} = 805,306,368$ sides. To determine the length of the side of each polygon accurately, he used results from trigonometry and an efficient algorithm for calculating square roots that had not been available to Archimedes.

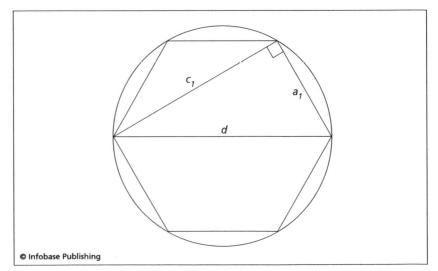

Al-Kāshī used the relationships between the sides and chords of polygons inscribed in circles to estimate the value of π to 16 decimal places.

From the right triangle formed by the side (a_n) of the inscribed polygon with $3 \cdot 2^n$ sides, its associated chord (c_n), and the diameter of the circle ($d = 2r$), al-Kāshī produced the equation $a_n = \sqrt{(2r)^2 - c_n^2}$. He also discovered a formula, $c_n = \sqrt{2(2r + c_{n-1})}$, that allowed him to calculate the length of the chord c_n from the length of the chord c_{n-1} in the inscribed polygon having half as many sides. Starting with a six-sided polygon whose chord and side had lengths $c_1 = r\sqrt{3}$ and $a_1 = r$, his two formulas produced the sequence of values:

$$c_2 = r\sqrt{2+\sqrt{3}} \qquad\qquad a_2 = r\sqrt{2-\sqrt{3}}$$

$$c_3 = r\sqrt{2+\sqrt{2+\sqrt{3}}} \qquad\qquad a_3 = r\sqrt{2-\sqrt{2+\sqrt{3}}}$$

$$c_4 = r\sqrt{2+\sqrt{2+\sqrt{2+\sqrt{3}}}} \qquad a_4 = r\sqrt{2-\sqrt{2+\sqrt{2+\sqrt{3}}}}$$

etc.

Because he had an efficient algorithm for precisely calculating square roots, al-Kāshī was able to produce 28 pairs of accurate computations. Multiplying the final result, a_{28}, by the number of sides in the corresponding polygon, he obtained the perimeter of the inscribed polygon with $3 \cdot 2^{28}$ sides. Through a similar sequence of computations, he obtained an estimate for the perimeter of the circumscribed polygon with $3 \cdot 2^{28}$ sides and used the average of these two values as his estimate for $2\pi r$, the circumference of the circle of radius r.

Throughout the entire process, al-Kāshī performed all his computations in sexagesimal notation with nine fractional digits presenting his estimate as $2\pi \approx 6{:}16, 59, 28, 1, 34, 51, 46, 14, 50$, a notation that represented the fractional sum

$$6 + \frac{16}{60} + \frac{59}{60^2} + \frac{28}{60^3} + \frac{1}{60^4} + \frac{34}{60^5} + \frac{51}{60^6} + \frac{46}{60^7} + \frac{14}{60^8} + \frac{50}{60^9}.$$

He converted this value to the corresponding base-10 format as the 16-digit decimal value $2\pi \approx 6.2831853071795865$. In both approximations, all the digits were correct, a significant improvement over the estimates provided by Archimedes and Ptolemy that were accurate to only three decimal places and those provided by the Indian mathematician Āryabhata in the sixth century and the Arab mathematician Muhammad al-Khwārizmī in the ninth century that had four digits of precision. Al-Kāshī's estimate for 2π and the corresponding estimate for $\pi \approx 3.1415926535897932$ were eventually surpassed in 1596, when German mathematician Ludolph van Ceulen used polynomials with $60 \cdot 2^{33}$ sides to determine the value of π to 20 decimal places.

Roots, Decimals, and Domes

Al-Kāshī's most well-known work was a five-volume set of books titled *Mifāh al-hisāb* (The key of arithmetic, also known as The reckoner's key). Completed on March 2, 1427, and dedicated to Bēg, this work was a compilation of elementary mathematics intended as a textbook for university students and as a manual for astronomers, land surveyors, architects, and merchants. Consistent with the title of the book, al-Kāshī demonstrated that the ability to solve diverse applications of algebra, geometry, and trigonometry ultimately depended on accurate computational techniques. His contemporaries and subsequent generations of scholars praised the book's pedagogical features and its broad range of applications. The book and an abbreviated version titled *Talkhīs al-Miftāh* (Compendium of the key) served as university texts and practical handbooks for several centuries.

In the first of the work's five books titled "On the arithmetic of integers," al-Kāshī described a commonly used method for estimating nth roots of numbers using the formula

$$\sqrt[n]{N} \approx a + \frac{N - a^n}{(a + 1)^n - a^n}$$, where a was the largest integer for which

$a^n < N$. In the process of computing the denominator, he presented the general formula for raising a sum of two terms to the nth power,

$$(a + b)^n = a^n + \binom{n}{1} a^{n-1}b + \binom{n}{2} a^{n-2}b^2 + \binom{n}{3} a^{n-3}b^3 + \ldots + b^n;$$

explained how to compute the necessary binomial coefficients $\binom{n}{1}$, $\binom{n}{2}$, $\binom{n}{3}$, etc. using the entries of Pascal's triangle; and presented the first nine rows of that structure. The binomial expansion and Pascal's triangle had been used throughout China and India for several centuries and had appeared with the formula for the nth root in Khayyám's 12th-century writings. As he had done in his earlier treatises, al-Kāshī thoroughly explained the computational techniques rhetorically (in words) because symbolic algebra (using variables and exponents) had not yet been introduced.

The second book, "On the arithmetic of fractions," explained how to represent fractional values in the base-10 decimal system of notation and how that format efficiently enabled one to perform arithmetical computations. Al-Kāshī presented two notations for representing decimal fractions: one using a vertical line to separate the integer and fractional parts of a number and the other writing the powers of 10 from the denominators above the fractional digits. With these conventions, the value 23.754 would have been represented as $23 | 754$ or as $2\ 3\ \overset{1\ 2\ 3}{7\ 5\ 4}$ meaning $23 + \dfrac{7}{10^1} + \dfrac{5}{10^2} + \dfrac{4}{10^3}$. Decimal fractions had been used by Chinese and Indian mathematicians and had appeared in Arabic works starting with the 10th-century writings of Abu'l Hasan al-Uqlīdisī. Al-Kāshī's contribution was to apply to decimal fractions the same methods of arithmetical computation that were used with decimal integers.

In the third book, "On the computation of astronomers," al-Kāshī explained how to use the sexagesimal system of notation for manipulating both whole number and fractional quantities. He convincingly argued that the decimal system in which each quantity was divided into 10 parts was superior to the sexagesimal system in which each quantity was divided into 60 parts because it enabled all computations to be made more efficiently. These methods of calculating with decimal fractions completed the development of the Hindu-Arabic number system. In the next two centuries, al-Kāshī's influential ideas on decimal computations spread to Turkey, throughout the Byzantine Empire, and into western Europe. Today the sexagesimal system continues to be used only for the measurement of angles in degrees, minutes (1/60th of a degree), and seconds (1/60th of a minute) and for the measurement of time with 60 minutes in each hour and 60 seconds in each minute.

"On the measurement of plane figures and bodies," the fourth section of the treatise, presented five methods for estimating areas and volumes of architectural arches, vaults, and *qubba* (domes) using only a straight-edge and compass. Elaborate Arabic architectural structures frequently consisted of a combination of plane and curved surfaces that needed to be plastered, painted, or gilded with gold leaf and were sometimes taxed according to the volumes they enclosed. Al-Kāshī devised methods for projecting the complicated three-dimensional surfaces into basic two-dimensional plane figures from which the original areas and volumes could be determined. The most challenging structure was the *muqarnas* (stalactite vault) in which a collection of diverse shapes hung from a wall, a column, or a ceiling. Al-Kāshī distinguished four types of *muqarnas* and systematically explained methods for resolving their surface areas and volumes.

The final book of the voluminous text was titled "On the solution of problems by means of algebra and the rule of two false assumptions." In this section of the work, al-Kāshī explained methods for solving linear and quadratic equations as well as systems of such equations. He showed how to use the popular technique of two false assumptions (also known as double-false position), by which an estimated but incorrect "solution" could be revised to produce a correct solution for many types of problems. He claimed that he had identified 70 types of fourth-degree equations with positive coefficients such as $ax^4 + dx + e = bx^3 + cx^2$ and that for each type of equation he had determined how to select two circles, parabolas, or hyperbolas whose point of intersection coincided with one of the positive roots of the given equation. Although he did not complete his proposed analysis, his brief comments represented the first attempt to create geometric solutions of fourth-degree algebraic equations systematically.

Estimating sin(1°)

Al-Kāshī's final mathematical treatise titled *Risāla al-watar wa'l-jaib* (Treatise on the chord and sine) was unfinished when he died in Samarkand on June 22, 1429. Qādī Zāde al-Rūmī, one of his colleagues from the observatory, completed the work soon after his death. In this treatise, al-Kāshī revealed an original iterative method by which he calculated the value of sin(1°) to 10 sexagesimal digits as 0:1, 2, 49, 43, 11, 14, 44, 16, 20, 17, representing the fractional sum

$$\frac{1}{60} + \frac{2}{60^2} + \frac{49}{60^3} + \frac{43}{60^4} + \frac{11}{60^5} + \frac{14}{60^6} + \frac{44}{60^7} + \frac{16}{60^8} + \frac{20}{60^9} + \frac{17}{60^{10}}.$$

He also gave the approximation with 18 decimal digits as 0.017452406437283571.

Starting with a well-known trigonometric formula used for finding the sine of three times an angle, al-Kāshī realized that $x = 60 \sin(1°)$ was the solution of the equation $60 \sin(3°) = 3x - \dfrac{4x^3}{60^2}$. Using traditional trigonometric formulas to estimate the value of $\sin(3°)$ with sufficient precision and isolating the unknown x, the equation produced a formula that, with sexagesimal digits, became $x = \dfrac{47, 6{:}8, 29, 53, 37, 3, 45 + x^3}{45,0}$. Knowing that the value of $x = 60 \sin(1°)$ was close to 1, al-Kāshī let $x = 1$ in the right-hand side of the equation and obtained the resulting approximation $x = 1{:}2 = 1 + \dfrac{2}{60}$. Substituting this value for x, he obtained the better estimate $x = 1{:}2, 49 = 1 + \dfrac{2}{60} + \dfrac{49}{60^2}$. After completing nine of these iterations and making the increasingly difficult computations that accompanied each step, he obtained his 10-sexagesimal digit estimate for $x = 60 \sin(1°)$ and the corresponding base-60 and base-10 estimates for $\sin(1°)$.

The ability to make accurate astronomical calculations depended on precise tables of trigonometric functions. The most crucial value in a trigonometric table was $\sin(1°)$ because it was used to calculate the sines of both larger and smaller angles. After al-Kāshī's death, Bēg used this value of $\sin(1°)$ to calculate sine and tangent tables for every minute of arc with results that were accurate to five sexagesimal places. He included these in his *Zij-i Sulatani* (Astronomical tables of the sultan), an expanded version of al-Kāshī's *Zīj-i Khaqāni* based on the work done by the scholars at the Samarkand Observatory. The elegance of al-Kāshī's method and the ease with which it produced accurate results led some mathematical commentators to regard it as one of the greatest achievements of medieval algebra. His iterative algorithms surpassed all similar techniques designed in Europe until the 19th century.

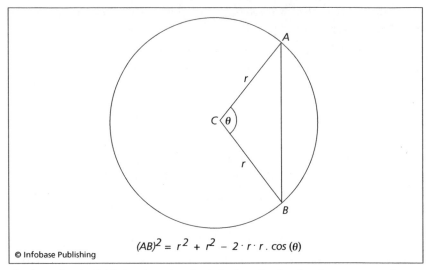

$$(AB)^2 = r^2 + r^2 - 2 \cdot r \cdot r \cdot \cos(\theta)$$

© Infobase Publishing

The formula al-Kāshī developed to find the length of a chord was a special case of the law of cosines known in French-speaking countries as al-Kāshī's theorem.

Al-Kāshī also presented a formula for determining the length of a chord, the line segment joining two points on the circumference of a circle. His formula specified that in a circle of radius r, a central angle of θ would cut off a chord of length $r\sqrt{2(1-\cos\theta)}$. Labeling the center of the circle as C and the endpoints of the chord as A and B, this formula can be rearranged as $(AB)^2 = r^2 + r^2 - 2 \cdot r \cdot r \cdot \cos\theta$. This result is a special case of the well-known law of cosines that states that in any triangle with sides of lengths a, b, and c, the sides are related by the equation $c^2 = a^2 + b^2 - 2 \cdot a \cdot b \cdot \cos\theta$. Although the third-century B.C.E. Greek mathematician Euclid proved an equivalent version of this formula in his book *Elements*, mathematicians in France still refer to the law of cosines as al-Kāshī's theorem.

Minor Works

In addition to his three major works on mathematics and his five earlier astronomical treatises, al-Kāshī produced five undated minor works on astronomy and the mathematics of computation. In *Ta'rīb al-zīj* (The Arabization of the astronomical table), he chronicled the historical changes and improvements that had been made to astronomical tables through the influence of generations of Arabic scholars. His *Wujūh al-'amal al'darb fi'l-takht wa'l-turāb* (Ways of multiplying by means of board and dust) explained how to use the popular dust board to make calculations with decimal numbers rather than using hand figures, mental calculations, or an abacus. He explained the interdependence of the values in tables of trigonometric functions and tables of planetary coordinates in the treatise *Miftāh al-asbāb fi 'ilm al-zīj* (The key of causes in the science of astronomical tables). In his third book on astronomical instruments, *Risāla dar sakht-i asturlāb* (Treatise on the construction of the astrolabe), he explained how to build an astrolabe, a sophisticated disk-shaped device that enabled mariners, travelers, and astronomers to determine their latitudes and longitudes from observing the angles between the horizon and fixed stars. For Muslims who followed the religious practice of facing the city of Mecca while reciting their daily prayers, his treatise *Risāla fī ma'rifa samt al-qibla min dāira hindiyya ma'rūfa* (Treatise on the determination of azimuth of the *qibla* by means of a circle known as Indian) explained how to determine the proper direction using an astronomical instrument invented in India.

Conclusion

Al-Kāshī distinguished himself as a creative mathematician who developed and used efficient methods for making accurate computations. The precision of his estimates for π and $\sin(1°)$ far exceeded those of all his predecessors. For each of these approximations, he introduced new techniques that demonstrated his exceptional insight and his advanced mathematical skills. He successfully argued for the computational superiority of the decimal system of fractions and developed useful methods for estimating areas and volumes of various architectural features.

FURTHER READING

O'Connor, J. J., and E. F. Robertson. "Ghiyath al-Din Jamshid Mas'ud al-Kashi," MacTutor History of Mathematics Archive, University of Saint Andrews. Available online.

URL: http://www-groups.dcs.st-andrews.ac.uk/~history/Mathe
maticians/Al-Kashi.html. Accessed January 24, 2005. Online
biography, from the University of Saint Andrews, Scotland.
Youschkevitch, A. P., and B. A. Rosenfeld. "al-Kāshī (or al-Kāshānī),
Ghiyāth al-Dīn Jamshīd Mas'ūd." In *Dictionary of Scientific
Biography*, vol. 7, edited by Charles C. Gillispie, 255–262. New
York: Scribner, 1972. Detailed encyclopedic biography with
extensive bibliography.

2

François Viète

(1540–1603)

François Viète introduced an influential system of notation for representing variables and constants. *(The Granger Collection)*

Father of Modern Algebra

The French mathematician François Viète (pronounced fran-SWAH vee-ET) introduced the convention of using vowels to represent variables and consonants to represent coefficients in algebraic equations. This innovation and the symbolic manipulations that it permitted transformed algebra into a systematic discipline that he called the analytic art. He introduced innovative algebraic, geometric, and trigonometric methods for solving equations of the second, third, and fourth degrees. He produced the first formula that gave an exact expression for using an infinite number of operations. His ability to decipher a coded message intended for the king of Spain earned him international notoriety.

Lawyer, Tutor, Government Official, and Code-Breaker

François Viète was born in 1540 at Fontenay-le-Comte in western France. He was also known in his mathematical writings by the Latinized versions of his name, Franciscus Vieta and Fransisci Vietae. The son of Étienne Viète and Marguerite Dupont, he followed his father into the legal profession, graduating from the University of Poitiers in 1560 with a law degree. During his professional career as an attorney, his well-known clients included Mary Stuart, Queen of Scots, and Henry of Navarre, who later became Henry IV, king of France.

In 1564, Viète accepted a position in the household of the prominent family of Jean de Parthenay and his wife, Antoinette d'Aubeterre. In fulfillment of his responsibilities as tutor for their daughter Catherine, he wrote a collection of essays on various scientific subjects. A compilation of several of these works published in 1637 under the title *Principes de cosmographie, tirés d'un manuscrit de Viette, et traduits en français* (Principles of cosmography, drawn from a manuscript of Viète and translated into French) included essays on the sphere, geography, and astronomy. During his three-year stint with the family, he also researched and wrote several private manuscripts, including "Mémoires de la vie de Jean de Parthenay Larchevêque" (Memoirs on the life of Jean de Parthenay Larchevêque) and "Généalogie de la maison de Parthenay" (Genealogy of the House of Parthenay).

From 1570 to 1602, Viète held a sequence of governmental posts as counselor to the parliament, master of requests, and royal privy counselor under three kings of France—Charles IX, Henry III, and Henry IV. In 1589, when the French army intercepted a coded message intended for Philip II, king of Spain, Viète spent five months analyzing the method of encryption. When he successfully deciphered the message, he reported his findings to Henry

IV in a document titled *Deschiffrement d'une lettre escripté par le Commandeur Moree au roi d'Espagne son maître* (Decipherment of a letter written by Commander Moree to his master the king of Spain). In addition to employing substitutions of individual letters, the intricate code utilized pairs of numbers and letters to represent more than 400 specific words. Believing that the code was unbreakable, Philip II accused Viète of using sorcery to crack the system of encryption.

Early Writings on Mathematics and Science

Viète, who never held a formal position as a mathematician, maintained an avid interest in the study of mathematics as an amateur throughout his lifetime. He enjoyed two periods of intensive mathematical study—the three years from 1564 to 1567, when he worked as Catherine de Parthenay's tutor, and the five years from 1584 to 1589, when his political enemies forced him out of the royal court.

During the first period of time and throughout the following decade, Viète devoted his mathematical efforts to the creation of an astronomy book titled *Ad harmonicon coeleste* (Toward celestial harmony). He completed the five-volume manuscript but never published the work because he became occupied with other projects. The book analyzed the planetary theories proposed by the second-century Egyptian astronomer Claudius Ptolemy, who believed that the Earth was the center of the universe, and the 16th-century Polish astronomer Nicolaus Copernicus, who proposed a Sun-centered universe. Viète's analysis concluded that the Ptolemaic system was superior because the Copernican system was not geometrically valid.

As part of this project, Viète wrote a lengthy treatise presenting the mathematical and astronomical background necessary to understand his analysis of the planetary models. In 1579, he published the first two books of this four-book set as *Canon mathematicus, seu ad triangula cum appendicibus* (Mathematical canon with an appendix on trigonometry). In the first book, he presented three tables of trigonometric functions, a table of values giving the integer lengths of the sides of selected right triangles, a table of products of the form $\dfrac{m \cdot n}{60}$ for all integers $0 < m < n < 60$, and a table of values related to calculations with the Egyptian calendar. The second book described the computational methods he used to construct the tables and explained how to solve plane and spherical triangles using trigonometric relations. In this second book, he also showed how to use trigonometry to determine the lengths of the sides of polygons with three, four, six, 10, and 15 sides that were inscribed in a circle. He completed but did not publish the two books on astronomical preliminaries.

Throughout his mathematical writings, Viète strongly advocated for the use of decimal fractions with denominators that were powers of 10 rather than the sexagesimal fractions with powers of 60 that astronomers had been using for centuries. In *Canon mathematicus*, Viète presented four possible notations for representing decimal fractions. He suggested writing 141,421,<u>356,24</u> for the value 141,421.35624, with the fractional part underlined and printed in smaller type than the integer part of the number. In other parts of his book, he represented the value 314,159.26535 as the mixed number 314,159 $\dfrac{265,35}{1,000,00}$ and as the **314,159**,265,35, using boldface print for the integer part. Later he wrote **99,946**|458,75 for the value 99,946.45875, with the integer part typed in boldface and the fractional part separated from it by a vertical line. Viète's use of decimal fractions contributed to their adoption throughout Europe as a replacement for sexagesimal fractions. Mathematicians were less willing to embrace the notations he suggested, preferring the now familiar decimal point that Italian mathematician G. A. Magini and German mathematician Christoph Clavius introduced in the 1590s to separate the integer and fractional parts of a number.

Modern Algebra Introduced as the Analytic Art

Viète made his most significant mathematical contribution through a group of books and manuscripts that mathematicians collectively refer to as *The Analytic Art*. He conceived his ideas during a productive period of unemployment in the 1580s and committed them to manuscript form during the following decade. He published some of his works immediately after completing them; others did not appear until years after his death.

In 1591, Viète published *In artem analyticem isagoge* (Introduction to the analytic art). He dedicated this landmark treatise on the subject of algebra to his former student Catherine de Parthenay. In this work, Viète introduced the convention of representing both known and unknown quantities in equations by letters. He used the vowels A, E, I, O, U, and Y to stand for unknown or variable quantities and used uppercase consonants to signify known or fixed quantities that he called coefficients. The standard practice at the time had been to use letters or words such as *cosa* (meaning "thing") to represent unknown quantities, utilize a combination of different symbols for their powers and roots, and write explicit numerical values for the coefficients and constants in the remaining parts of the equation. In order to explain a procedure for solving equations of a certain form, a mathematician typically described the process in words and illustrated it by solving several specific examples. The system of symbolic notation that Viète introduced enabled mathematicians to construct a general theory of equations. Rather than focusing on a specific equation, they could discuss entire classes of equations and could express methods of solution in general terms. They could also express in an abstract way the relationships between the solutions of an equation and the values of the coefficients. This vowel-and-consonant innovation, considered one of the most significant advances in the history of mathematics, prepared the way for the development of modern algebra.

Viète's book also introduced improved notation to denote repeated multiplication. He represented the second and third powers of the unknown value A by writing A *quadratus* (meaning "squared") and A *cubus* (meaning "cubed"). Compared to the notation introduced by the 15th-century Italian mathematician Rafael Bombelli in which these values were represented as Q and C or as 2 and 3 without any mention of the quantity that was repeatedly being multiplied, Viète's notation provided the advantage of being able to see relationships between the unknown value A and its powers rather than representing them as distinct quantities.

Mathematicians throughout Europe used Viète's vowel-and-consonant system as well as his notation for powers until 1637, when French mathematician René Descartes published *Discours de la méthode pour bien conduire sa raison et chercher la vérité dans les sciences* (Discourse on the method for rightly directing one's reason and searching for truth in the sciences) and the accompanying mathematical appendix *La géométrie* (The geometry). In these influential treatises, Descartes built on Viète's ideas by introducing the modern convention of using lowercase letters from the beginning of the alphabet to denote known quantities and lowercase letters from the end of the alphabet for variables. Descartes also introduced the familiar exponential notation in which the square and the cube of the quantity x were represented as x^2 and x^3, respectively.

The system of symbolic notation Viète introduced allowed him to redefine the meaning and purpose of algebra. He introduced the phrase "the analytic art" to show that algebra was the means by which one could search for mathematical truths, a goal that he likened to the analysis performed by the ancient Greeks. In this "science of correct discovery," he distinguished three kinds of analysis: *zetetics* and *poristics* that had been used by the Greeks and a new type of analysis known as *exegetics*. Zetetic analysis described the process of transforming a problem into an equation or proportion relating the known and unknown quantities. Poristic analysis was the manipulation of symbols performed in the process of proving or illustrating a theorem. Exegetic analysis meant the manipulation of the symbols in an equation or proportion in order to determine the value of the unknown quantity.

Viète presented a detailed and improved process of symbolic algebraic manipulations. He identified rules for rewriting and solving equations including *antithesis*, moving terms from one side of the equation to the other side; *hypobibasm*, dividing all the terms in an equation by a common factor; and *parabolism*, converting an equation into a proportion. In order to satisfy his fundamental law of homogeneity that required all terms in an equation to have the same "genus" (dimension), he introduced artificial coefficients with the necessary compensating powers. Although this practice was cumbersome, it enabled him to introduce the method of *logistice speciosa* (calculation with unspecified quantities) that allowed the rules of algebra to be applied in the same way to numbers and to geometric magnitudes—ideas that the Greeks had regarded as distinct processes. Calling Viète's system of symbolic manipulation logistic analysis and the new algebra, European mathematicians recognized its potential as a powerful, generalized method for representing and solving problems.

In 1593, Viète published further details about the analytic art in *Zeteticorum libri quinque* (Five books on zetetics). This treatise explained how to use the methods of algebra to create and solve proportions for a variety of problems involving means, triangles, and squares. The work also presented algebraic methods for solving classical problems in which one was asked to determine the values of two quantities from information about their sum, their ratio, or the sum of their squares. In this book, Viète suggested new notations for roots, using L from the Latin word *latus* (meaning "side") for square root and LC from the Latin *latus cubus* (meaning "side of a cube") for cube root. With these notations, $L64 = \sqrt{64} = 8$ represented the length of the side of a square having an area of 64, and $LC64 = \sqrt[3]{64} = 4$ gave the length of the edge of a cube having a volume of 64. These notations, together with Viète's concepts of genus and homogeneity, showed the strong influence geometry exerted on the development of his algebraic methods, terminology, and symbolism.

Theory of Equations Provides Diverse Methods of Solution

Viète's literal notation and his methods for manipulating algebraic expressions enabled him to develop systematic approaches for equations. He constructed a general theory of equations by which one could algebraically convert various types of equations into a small number of standard forms and then use algebraic, geometric, or trigonometric techniques to solve those canonical forms. Explanations of his methods appeared in the treatise *Supplementum geometriae* (Supplement on geometry) that he published in 1593 and in two manuscripts that were not published until 1615 in the posthumous work *Francisci Vietae fontenaensis de aequationum recognitione et emendatione tractotus duo* (François Viète of Fontenay: Two treatises on the recognition and emendation of equations). These works presented his methods for solving quadratic (second-degree), cubic (third-degree), and quartic (fourth-degree) equations.

To solve quadratic equations, Viète identified various relationships that existed between the coefficients and the solutions. He explained one of these relations for second-degree equations that, in modern notation, could be rewritten in the standard form $x^2 - bx + c = 0$. After converting the given equation to this form, it could be solved by finding two numbers that added up to b and multiplied to c. For equations that could be rewritten as $x^2 + bx = c$, he showed that the substitution $x = y - \dfrac{b}{2}$ would convert the equation to the form $y^2 = c - \dfrac{3b^2}{4}$. This equation, in which the variable appeared only once, could then be solved by taking the square root of both sides.

Using an approach similar to his methods for solving quadratic equations, Viète explained how to reduce all cubic equations to three standard forms and gave routine methods for solving those canonical forms. A typical reduction used an algebraic substitution such as $x = y - a/3$ to reduce an equation of the form $x^3 + ax^2 + bx + c = 0$ to the simpler standard form $x^3 + dx + e = 0$, which had no x^2 term. Using two more substitutions, this equation could be reduced to a quadratic equation whose solutions provided the answers to the original equation. These widely used reduction techniques became known as "Viète's substitutions."

To solve cubic equations that could be written in the standard form $x^3 - bx = c$, Viète used the method of two mean proportionals. With an example such as $x^3 - 4x = 192$, this method required the solver to find two numbers m and n between $\sqrt{4} = 2$ and $\dfrac{192}{4} = 48$ that satisfied the proportions $\dfrac{2}{m} = \dfrac{m}{n} = \dfrac{n}{m + 48}$. Obtaining the mean proportionals $m = 6$ and $n = 18$ using well-known methods provided $x = m = 6$ as a solution of the original cubic equation.

Viète also showed how to solve cubic equations by a method of trigonometric substitutions. For certain equations of the form

$x^3 - 3b^2x = b^2d$, the substitutions $x = 2b \cos(\theta)$ and $d = 2b \cos(3\theta)$ produced a trigonometric equation that represented a well-known relationship between two right triangles. Solving the right triangles with the help of trigonometric tables efficiently produced the solution to the original cubic equation.

The fourth technique Viète used to solve cubic equations showed his deep understanding of the direct relationships that existed between coefficients and roots. For cubic equations of the form $x^3 - ax^2 + bx - c = 0$ with roots r_1, r_2, and r_3, he showed that the three coefficients and the three roots had to satisfy the equations $a = r_1 + r_2 + r_3$, $b = r_1r_2 + r_1r_3 + r_2r_3$ and $c = r_1r_2r_3$. The solutions of these simpler equations produced the roots of the original cubic equation. In the 1620s, French mathematician Albert Girard showed that with the appropriate plus or minus sign the general form of these equations, known as "Viète's formulas," applied to the coefficients and roots in all polynomial equations.

For quartic equations, Viète gave algebraic substitutions that reduced a given equation into one of the standard forms and showed how to solve these canonical forms by reducing them to a pair of quadratic equations. He also derived a set of four equations similar to the cubic Viète's formulas to relate the coefficients and the roots of certain quartic equations.

Viète's approach to solving equations represented an improvement over the work of earlier mathematicians because his vowel-and-consonant system of notation allowed him to identify fewer standard forms and to exhibit relationships between solutions and coefficients more efficiently. Since he required all coefficients to be positive and considered roots to be meaningful only if they were positive numbers, he did not appreciate the full potential of these general techniques. Nevertheless, his books introducing the analytic art established Viète's reputation as one of the leading mathematicians in France.

Further Advances in Geometry, Trigonometry, and Algebra

In his other mathematical works, Viète contributed new methods, ideas, and insights to several branches of mathematics. In 1592, he gave a series of public lectures refuting French mathematician

J. J. Scaliger's claim that he had found ruler-and-compass methods to square the circle, trisect an angle, and construct the two mean proportionals between two line segments. Viète's presentation of his arguments was so effective that Scaliger left the country, with his reputation as a scholar severely tarnished.

The following year, Viète published an extensive treatise titled *Variorum de rebus mathematicis* (Collection of mathematical refutations) in which he provided his proofs explaining why these ruler-and-compass constructions were not possible and presented several other techniques and ideas related to classical Greek geometry. He showed how to identify seven equally spaced points on the circumference of a circle and construct an inscribed regular heptagon. By constructing an inscribed polygon with $6 \cdot 2^{16} = 393,216$ sides, he correctly estimated the value of the constant π to nine decimal places as 3.141592653. He also showed how to find the tangent line at any point on an Archimedean spiral.

In this treatise, Viète presented two ideas dealing with infinity that gave evidence of his mature level of insight into this mathematical concept. Explaining that a circle is a regular polygon with infinitely many straight sides, he argued that any line that touches a circle does not form an angle with the circle because it

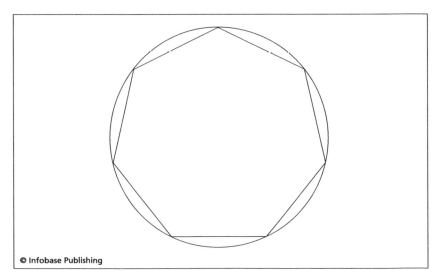

Viète explained how to construct an inscribed regular heptagon.

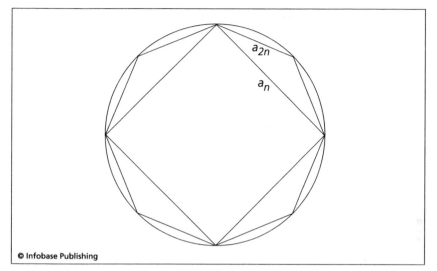

By studying the relationships between the lengths of the sides of inscribed polygons with n sides and $2n$ sides, Viète expressed the constant π as an infinite product of square roots.

must coincide with one of those straight lines. This novel argument stated clearly the meaning of the angle of tangency and used the concept of infinity in a manner that had not been understood by other mathematicians. In another situation involving circles, Viète analyzed the pattern of calculations corresponding to an infinite sequence of inscribed polygons with $4 \cdot 2^n$ sides. By examining the ratios of the perimeters of successive polygons, he produced a formula that expressed the exact value of π as

$$\pi = \frac{2}{\left(\sqrt{\frac{1}{2}}\right) \cdot \left(\sqrt{\frac{1}{2}+\frac{1}{2}\sqrt{\frac{1}{2}}}\right) \cdot \left(\sqrt{\frac{1}{2}+\frac{1}{2}\sqrt{\frac{1}{2}+\frac{1}{2}\sqrt{\frac{1}{2}}}}\right) \cdots} \quad .$$

Where all prior attempts to estimate the value of π used finitely many terms to produce approximations of varying precision, Viète's achievement marked the first successful attempt to give an exact expression for π using an infinite number of operations.

In this rich treatise, Viète also explained the recently discovered method of computation known as *prosthaphaeresis*. In the previous decade, a collection of German astronomers and mathematicians including Christoph Clavius and Joost Bürgi had developed this efficient technique that enabled one to multiply two numbers by adding two related values. Viète explained how the relationships between trigonometric functions produced a set of formulas including $\cos(A) \cdot \cos(B) = \dfrac{\cos(A + B) + \cos(A - B)}{2}$ and

$\sin(A) \cdot \sin(B) = \dfrac{\cos(A - B) - \cos(A + B)}{2}$. Using one of these formulas

and a table of trigonometric functions, he showed that one could multiply two numbers x and y by finding the angles A and B for which $x = \cos(A)$ and $y = \cos(B)$, retrieving the values of $\cos(A + B)$ and $\cos(A - B)$ from the table and adding their values together. Although Viète did not discover these formulas, their inclusion in a widely read treatise written by a mathematician of his stature helped to popularize their use.

Viète's investigations of the geometrical relationships between trigonometric functions led him to develop formulas that expressed $\sin(n\theta)$ and $\cos(n\theta)$ in terms of the simpler quantities $\sin(\theta)$ and $\cos(\theta)$ for $2 \le n \le 10$. The double-angle and triple-angle formulas in this collection had been known to the ancient Greeks, but the more general formulas first appeared in Viète's treatise *Ad angularium sectionum analyticem* (About sectioning angles analytically), which was written in the 1590s but not published until 1615. He presented each multiple-angle formula as a polynomial in powers of $\sin(\theta)$ and $\cos(\theta)$, with the coefficients of each term corresponding to the coefficients of the expansion

$$(x + y)^n = x^n + nx^{n-1} y + \frac{n(n - 1)}{1 \cdot 2} x^{n-2}y^2 + \cdots + y^n.$$ In modern ter-

minology, these values are known as the binomial coefficients

$$\binom{n}{0} = 1, \binom{n}{1} = n, \binom{n}{2} = \frac{n(n - 1)}{1 \cdot 2}, \cdots, \binom{n}{n} = 1.$$

In 1593, Henry IV sought Viète's assistance when Belgian mathematician Adriaan van Roomen challenged all mathematicians in France to solve the equation

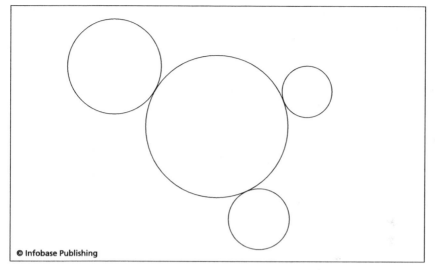

After finding the 23 positive solutions to Adriaan van Roomen's equation, Viète challenged him to construct a circle that was tangent to three given circles, a classic geometric problem suggested by the ancient Greek mathematician Apollonius.

$x^{45} - 45x^{43} + 945x^{41} - \cdots - 3795x^3 + 45x = K$. Viète discovered one solution within minutes of reading the problem and produced the other 22 positive solutions the following day. Recognizing that the problem was related to the expansion of $\sin(45\theta)$ and that $45 = 3 \cdot 3 \cdot 5$, he used his angle-sectioning technique to solve two third-degree and one fifth-degree equations and generate all the positive solutions. In 1595, Viète published his method of solution in the treatise *Ad problema, quod omnibus mathematicis totius orbis construendum proposuit Adrianus Romanus, responsum* (Response to a problem proposed by Adrianus Romanus that brought together eminent mathematicians throughout the whole world). At end of this work, he challenged van Roomen to solve the classic problem of using a ruler and compass to construct a circle that is tangent to three given circles. In 1600, after van Roomen produced a solution using two hyperbolas, Viète shared his ruler-and-compass solution with his colleague. Impressed by the abilities Viète demonstrated in solving the two problems, van Roomen traveled to Fontenay to spend a month with him, and the two became close friends.

In 1600, Viète produced *De numerosa potestatum purarum* (On the pure power of numbers), one of the last of his publications to appear during his lifetime. In this work, he explained a method that used successive approximations to obtain solutions to polynomial equations. This iterative technique used an approximate value to obtain the first digit of the solution. Each additional step of the repetitive process of substitution and algebraic simplification produced one more digit of the numerical solution. Viète's technique was similar to the method now known as Horner's method, although Viète restricted his attention to exact integer solutions while the modern technique obtains decimal approximations as well.

Conclusion

When François Viète died on February 23, 1603, two months after retiring from public service in the royal court of Henry IV, he left behind a large collection of mathematical writings. In 1615, his Scottish colleague Alexander Anderson assembled and printed several of his unpublished manuscripts. In 1646, Dutch mathematician Frans van Schooten edited his collected works and published them under the title *Opera mathematica* (Mathematical works).

By the time his collected works appeared, the mathematical community had embraced and improved upon most of Viète's ideas and techniques. His notational system of vowels and consonants to represent unknown and known quantities in equations was a significant and widely accepted innovation that enabled mathematicians to develop general methods for solving classes of similar equations. The vowel-and-consonant concept was an important idea that Descartes generalized in his notational system of 1637. Viète's recognition of the relationships between the coefficients and the solutions of polynomial equations led to the development of a general theory of equations that became the central focus of study in 17th- and 18th-century algebra. His techniques for sectioning angles emphasized relationships between algebra, geometry, and trigonometry that mathematicians continue to study today in the branch of mathematics known as algebraic geometry. Although his analytic art and logistic analysis no longer constitute "the new algebra," Viète's innovative method of thinking in more general and formal terms advanced mathematics toward modern algebra and the study of symbolic structure.

FURTHER READING

Boyer, Carl, and Uta Merzbach. *A History of Mathematics.* 2nd ed. New York: Wiley, 1991. Chapter 16 frames Viète's algebraic innovations in relation to the work of his predecessors, contemporaries, and successors.

Busard, H. L. L. "Viète, François." In *Dictionary of Scientific Biography,* vol. 14, edited by Charles C. Gillispie, 18–25. New York: Scribner, 1972. Encyclopedic biography including detailed descriptions of the content of many of his books.

O'Connor, J. J., and E. F. Robertson. "François Viète," MacTutor History of Mathematics Archive, University of Saint Andrews. Available online. URL: http://www-groups.dcs.st-andrews.ac.uk/~history/Mathematicians/Viete.html. Accessed June 3, 2005. Online biography, from the University of Saint Andrews, Scotland.

3

John Napier

(1550–1617)

John Napier published the first table of logarithms that simplified the process of computation. *(Library of Congress)*

Coinventor of Logarithms

The amateur Scottish mathematician John Napier (pronounced NAY-pee-yur) simplified the process of computation when he published the first table of logarithms. His influential books helped to popularize the use of the decimal point as an efficient notation for separating the integer and fractional parts of a number. Napier's bones, one of several computational devices he invented, became a popular tool for making the process of multiplying large numbers more efficient. In addition to his mathematical contributions, the "marvelous Merchiston" developed improved methods of agriculture and sketched designs for a submarine and other military weapons.

Inventor and Theologian

John Napier, the eighth laird of Merchiston, was born in 1550 at Merchiston Castle, his family's estate in Edinburgh, Scotland. He was the eldest son of Sir Archibald Napier and his first wife, Janet Bothwell, the daughter of an Edinburgh burgess. As the title laird indicates, the Napiers were wealthy members of the gentry class (the lowest class of nobility) owning property in Edinburgh, Lennox, Menteith, and Gartness. Working in the service of the king of Scotland, as his ancestors had done for generations, Sir Archibald held the office of justice-deputy, was knighted in 1565, and became Master of the Mint in 1582.

The spelling of John Napier's first and last names evolved over time. His first name appeared on the covers of his books as Jhone, John, Joannis, and Joanne, while his family name was variously rendered as Naipper, Napare, Napeir, Naper, Naperi, Nepair, Nepeir, Neper, Nepero, and Neperus. During his lifetime, he signed official documents as Jhone Neper, John Napeir, and Jhone Nepair. All modern references to him in mathematical literature use the spelling that his family has now adopted—John Napier.

At the age of 13, Napier enrolled at St. Salvator's College of St. Andrew's University in Fife, Scotland, where he developed an interest in theology. During his first year at school, his mother died, and he soon discontinued his studies. On the advice of his uncle, Adam Bothwell, bishop of Orkney, he traveled to continental Europe to pursue further education. By 1571, he had returned to Edinburgh having acquired an advanced knowledge of mathematics and classical literature. In 1572, Napier married Elizabeth Stirling, whose family owned the property adjacent to the Napier's Gartness estate. The couple resided in a castle that they built at Gartness and had two children, Archibald and Jane. After his first wife died in 1579, he married his second wife, Agnes Chisholm, with whom he had five sons and five daughters. In 1608, when his father died, he inherited the castle at Merchiston where he resided for the last nine years of his life.

Napier earned a reputation as an innovator and an inventor in a variety of fields. In agriculture, he experimented with the use of common salts to help kill weeds and to fertilize the soil in his fields. This technique was so effective that he published his findings in a book titled *The new order of gooding and manuring all sorts of field land with common salt*, and the government granted a monopoly to his family for this mode of tillage. He also earned a monopoly for his design of a hydraulic screw with a revolving axle that could be used to draw water out of coal pits. This device improved on the design of the Archimedean screw invented by the Greek mathematician Archimedes of Syracuse in the third century B.C.E. Napier developed an expertise in mensuration (measurement) and worked as a consultant helping to measure property for a number of landowners. In 1596, he circulated a brief manuscript titled *Secrete inventionis* (Secret inventions), in which he described his designs for four machines having military applications and discussed his experience with some of the prototypes that he had built. These machines included a round, armored chariot with holes through which the occupants could fire weapons in any direction, a submarine that could shoot projectiles underwater, a rapid-fire artillery gun capable of killing enemy soldiers and their horses, and a mirror that could focus the rays of the sun onto enemy ships to set them afire (another idea inspired by Archimedes). His many inventions and the esteem that his later publications garnered led his countrymen to refer to him as the "marvelous Merchiston."

In 1593, Napier, a staunch Presbyterian, published the results of his five years of theological research on the biblical Book of Revelations under the title *A plaine discovery of the whole revelation of St. John*. In this book, he delivered a passionate attack on Catholicism, concluding that the pope was the antichrist. He dedicated his writings to James VI, king of Scotland, who later became James I, king of England, and encouraged the king to scrutinize the religious loyalties of the members of his court. The book was widely read throughout Protestant Europe, and its translations into French, German, and Dutch required multiple printings to satisfy the demand.

Rumored to Be a Magician

Several events in Napier's life as well as his personal habits led his contemporaries to suspect that he had magical powers. They accused him of casting a spell on a flock of birds, employing a magic rooster to catch a thief, and using supernatural powers to locate buried treasure. These claims, together with his ability to grow superior crops, his habit of walking around his property in a long robe, and his preference for living a quiet, solitary lifestyle, led many observers to conclude that he was a magician.

The details surrounding these incidents and personality traits showed that Napier possessed exceptional mental abilities and made ingenious use of logic. In order to capture a flock of doves that had repeatedly eaten the seeds he had planted, he soaked a batch of seeds in alcohol and scattered them across his field. The next morning he gathered dozens of semiconscious birds and held them for ransom until their owner repaid him for the seeds they had eaten. To discover which of his servants had been stealing from him, he required each one to go into a dark room and briefly hold his pet rooster whose feathers he had covered with black soot. By inspecting the servants' hands, he determined that the guilty individual was the one whose hands were still clean because he had not touched the rooster. In 1594, Napier agreed to use the powers of his mind to locate a treasure that had been hidden at Fastcastle in Berwickshire. Although he signed a contract to conduct the search for Robert Logan of Restalrig, it is doubtful that he ever engaged in the treasure hunt. And the abundance of Napier's crops was due to his use of his scientifically developed fertilizing techniques.

Napier's penchant for roaming and his preference for solitude reflected his work habits as an amateur mathematician. He never held a formal position as a researcher or as a teacher. He was not part of a mathematical community and did not correspond with professional mathematicians or scholars. Working alone at his castle, Napier frequently wandered around his estate deep in thought as he pondered mathematical questions. Insisting on uninterrupted quiet when he focused on his mathematics, he would ask the miller operating the nearby grain mill to stop the waterwheel so that the clacking sound it made would not disrupt his concentration.

Napier's Bones Aid in Multiplication

Throughout his adult life, Napier maintained an interest in developing techniques and devices that would simplify the process of computation. In the early 1570s, shortly after he returned from Europe, he wrote his first mathematical treatise. In this five-part work that dealt primarily with arithmetic and algebra, he explained efficient methods of computation, described economical algebraic notations, and investigated imaginary roots of equations. He used the words *abundant* and *defective* to refer to positive and negative quantities, two ideas that had not yet matured and for which terminology had not yet been standardized. Had these thoughts been published at the time, this work would have contributed to the advancement of algebra. The uncirculated treatise remained in manuscript form until 1839, when one of his descendants published it under the name *De arte logistica* (On the logistical method). By that time, the ideas it presented had been discovered and superseded by other mathematicians.

Over a period of 45 years, Napier developed three mechanical methods for efficiently performing arithmetical computations. In 1617, he published detailed descriptions of these methods in a book titled *Rabdologiae* (Rabdology). He dedicated the book to Chancellor Seton, earl of Dunfermline. The book's title reflected the name he gave to the method of making arithmetical calculations using a set of numbered rods he had designed. Known as Napier's rods, Napier's bones, or simply as Napiers, each set of computational tools consisted of rectangular rods made of wood, ivory, or bone. Each of the four sides of a rod was inscribed with the first 10 multiples of one of the numbers 0, 1, 2, 3, …, 9. To multiply two numbers, such as 237 times 5, one would line up the rods for the digits 2, 3, and 7 next to each other and then combine the two-digit numbers in the fifth square on each rod by adding the leftmost digit of one value with the rightmost digit of its neighbor. The rods reduced the process of multiplication to the much simpler operation of addition that most people were able to perform. The book also explained how to use the rods to perform division and extraction of roots. Sets of these rods circulated widely throughout Europe and became popular with bookkeepers, accountants, and schoolchildren.

The second section of *Rabdologiae* described a calculating machine Napier had invented called a promptuary and the method of using it to multiply numbers, a process he called *promptuarium multiplicationis* (multiplication using a promptuary). A promptuary consisted of a set of metal plates inscribed with numbers and arranged in a box. By turning the plates in the prescribed manner, one could readily multiply two numbers. Although more complicated and costly than a set of Napier's rods, this calculating device had the advantage of the machine performing the complete computation without the user having to add partial results or keep track of carry digits. The promptuary was one of the earliest-known calculating machines, but it did not enjoy widespread acceptance.

In the appendix of *Rabdologiae*, Napier described a method of performing arithmetical computations that he called local arithmetic. After showing how to use markers on a chessboard to represent positive integers as sums of powers of two, he explained how to use this positional binary notation to add, subtract, multiply, divide, and take square roots. The process he described was quite similar to the methods that modern computers use to represent and manipulate numbers. If efficient notations for exponents and base-2 numbers had existed at the time, this innovative method of computation might have contributed to the development of efficient calculating machines.

Logarithms Simplify Computation

During the period of years from 1590 until his death in 1617, Napier developed his most important mathematical contribution— the concept of logarithms. He explained his system of logarithms in a pair of books that appeared in print in the opposite order that he had written them. In 1614, he published *Mirifici logarithmorum canonis descriptio* (*Description of an Admirable Table of Logarithms*) and dedicated the work to Prince Charles, who later became Charles I, king of Scotland. In this treatise, Napier explained how to use logarithms to solve problems involving triangles and presented a detailed table of logarithms. In 1619, two years after Napier's death, his son Robert transcribed and published the companion book, *Mirifici logarithmorum canonis constructio* (Construction of

In his 1614 treatise, *Mirifici logarithmorum canonis descriptio* (Description of an admirable table of logarithms), Napier introduced the first table of logarithms. *(Library of Congress)*

an admirable table of logarithms), in which he explained the geometric basis for the values of logarithms and the process by which he had constructed the table of logarithms.

Napier had originally called logarithms artificial numbers and used that terminology throughout *Constructio*. By the time he wrote *Descriptio*, he had created the word *logarithm* from a combination of the Greek words *logos* (ratio) and *arithmos* (number). For each angle θ from 0° to 45°, his massive table of logarithms presented the values of sin θ, cos θ, log sin θ, log cos θ, and log tan θ. The 90-page table included values for 2,700 angles measured in increments of a minute (1/60th of a degree) and specified the five calculated values with seven digits of accuracy.

In *Descriptio*, Napier explained that his logarithms had the fundamental property that if four quantities a, b, c, and d had the relationship $\dfrac{a}{b} = \dfrac{c}{d}$, then their logarithms satisfied the equation $\log a - \log b = \log c - \log d$. He then showed how, without having to multiply, divide, or calculate square roots, one could use this property to find the measures of the angles in a right triangle when the lengths of two of the sides were known. For example, in a right triangle with hypotenuse c, if the side opposite angle A had length a, then the angle and the two sides would be related by the equation $\log \sin A = \log a - \log c$. For triangles that did not include a right angle, Napier showed how his logarithms reduced the law of sines $\dfrac{\sin A}{a} = \dfrac{\sin B}{b}$ to the equation $\log \sin A - \log a = \log \sin B - \log b$.

In situations where one knew two sides and the angle opposite one of them or two angles and the side opposite one of them, the

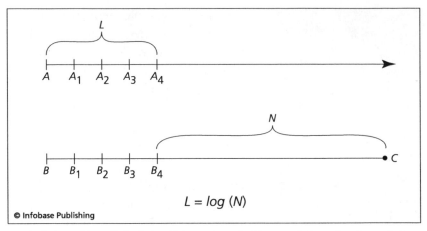

$$L = log (N)$$

Napier's logarithms linked the distance traveled by a point moving from A at a constant speed (L) to the distance remaining to be traveled by a point moving from B toward C at a reducing rate of speed (N). He related these arithmetic and geometric progressions by the equation L = log N.

logarithmic version of the law of sines made it possible to determine the fourth quantity by simply adding and subtracting the appropriate logarithms. He similarly explained how logarithms reduced the law of tangents

$$\frac{a+b}{a-b} = \frac{\tan\left(\dfrac{A+B}{2}\right)}{\tan\left(\dfrac{A-B}{2}\right)}$$ to the more efficient logarithmic identity

$$\log(a + b) - \log(a - b) = \log \tan \left(\frac{A + B}{2}\right) - \log \tan \left(\frac{A - B}{2}\right).$$

Given the lengths of two sides of a triangle, a and b, and the measure of the angle C between them, one could solve for the other two angles A and B using this logarithmic identity and the relation $A + B = 180° - C$.

In *Constructio*, Napier explained how he constructed his table of logarithms by relating the distances traveled by two points moving along two straight lines. The first point traveled at a uniform speed covering equal distances in equal times. The second point traveled toward a fixed point at a decreasing rate of speed that was proportional to the distance remaining to be traveled. Letting the two points start at the same time with the same initial speed, letting L represent the distance traveled by the first point, and letting N represent the distance remaining to be traveled by the second point, Napier gave his definition of logarithm as $L = \log N$. Since he assumed his second point started $10^7 = 10,000,000$ units distant from the fixed point, Napier's definition of $L = \log N$ implied that L and N were related by the equation $10,000,000(.9999999)^L = N$ or

$$10^7 \left(1 - \frac{1}{10^7}\right)^L = N.$$

Logarithms Receive International Acclaim

Henry Briggs, professor of geometry at London's Gresham College, immediately recognized the significance of Napier's concept of logarithms. During his monthlong visits to Napier's home in 1615 and 1616, the two mathematicians revised the scale of the system of logarithms, making $\log 1 = 0$ and $\log 10 = 1$. This improved system of logarithms, known today as common logarithms or base-10 logarithms, had the additional properties that $\log(ab) = \log a + \log b$,

$\log \left(\dfrac{a}{b}\right) = \log a - \log b$, and $\log(a^b) = b \log a$. Briggs published the

results of their joint work and the first table of these common logarithms in his 1617 book, *Logarithmorum chilias prima* (Logarithms of the first 1,000 numbers). This table became the basis for all tables of logarithms constructed into the 20th century.

Napier's introduction of the concept of logarithms and the publication of the first tables of logarithms had an immediate and widespread impact on mathematics and astronomy. Edward Wright's 1616 English translation of *Descriptio* disseminated Napier's ideas on logarithms to a wider audience. John Speidell's 1619 *New Logarithms* presented a variation on Napier's concept that became known as natural logarithms based on the constant e whose value is approximately 2.71828. Although Napier had not envisioned logarithms as powers of a radix or base, his original logarithms were essentially logarithms with base $1/e$. German astronomer Johannes Kepler dedicated his 1620 *Ephemerides* to Napier, stating that the invention of logarithms was the central idea that enabled him to discover the third law of planetary motion. Kepler and other astronomers recognized the efficiency of using logarithms to make computations with large numbers and rapidly adopted logarithms as the standard method of computation in astronomy.

As the use of logarithms became popular throughout Europe, three English inventors produced mechanical calculating devices calibrated with logarithmic scales. In 1624, astronomer Edmund Gunter, one of Briggs's colleagues at Gresham College, invented Gunter's scale—a single two-foot ruler marked in logarithmic units that enabled one to multiply numbers by adding their logarithms with the use of a pair of dividers. During the next eight years, mathematicians Richard Delamain and William Oughtred both invented circular slide rules consisting of a pair of metal circles attached at their centers and inscribed on their edges with logarithmic scales that could be turned to add the logarithms of two numbers. In 1632, Oughtred invented the linear slide rule in which two Gunter scales slid next to each other, eliminating the need for dividers. Slide rules rapidly gained in popularity and enjoyed widespread use. For more than three centuries, they were the most commonly used computational device for making mathematical, scientific, and engineering calculations until handheld calculators made them obsolete in the 1970s.

Joost Bürgi, a Swiss mathematician working in Germany, independently invented the concept of logarithms during the same period of years that Napier worked. In his version of logarithm, if $100,000,000(1.0001)^L = N$ he called $10L$ the red number that corresponded to the black number N. Bürgi's concept used the same fundamental principles as Napier's with different values and terminology and without the geometric motivation. He published his ideas in the form of a table of antilogarithms in the 1620 book *Arithmetische und geometrische Progress-Tabulen* (Tables of arithmetic and geometric progression). Although Napier published his work

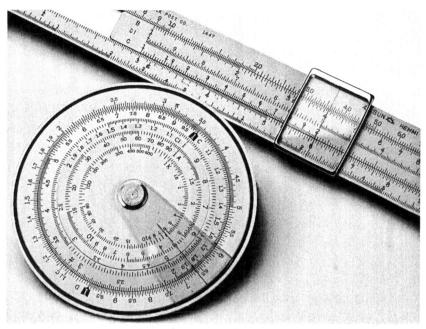

Circular and linear slide rules designed with movable logarithmic scales remained popular calculating devices until the 1970s. *(Courtesy of Dr. Warren Kay and Dr. Charles Kay. Photograph by Kevin Salemme)*

before Bürgi did, mathematicians generally regard the two as coinventors of the concept of logarithms.

Additional Mathematical Contributions

In addition to the concept of logarithms, Napier's books *Descriptio* and *Constructio* contained several other mathematical ideas. In both books, as well as in *Rabdologaie*, he advocated for the use of a period or a comma as an efficient notation for separating the integer and fractional parts of a number. Simon Stevin in Belgium and G. A. Magini and Christoph Clavius in Germany had used similar notation in the 1580s and 1590s, but their use had not become widespread. The international popularity and influence of Napier's *Constructio* resulted in the standard use of the decimal point throughout Europe.

A set of four formulas used in spherical trigonometry known as Napier's formulas or Napier's analogies first appeared in *Constructio*.

In a spherical triangle with sides a, b, and c and angles A, B, and C, these formulas state the relationships:

$$\frac{\sin\left(\dfrac{a-b}{2}\right)}{\sin\left(\dfrac{a+b}{2}\right)} = \frac{\tan\left(\dfrac{A-B}{2}\right)}{\tan\left(\dfrac{C}{2}\right)} \qquad \frac{\cos\left(\dfrac{a-b}{2}\right)}{\cos\left(\dfrac{a+b}{2}\right)} = \frac{\tan\left(\dfrac{A+B}{2}\right)}{\tan\left(\dfrac{C}{2}\right)}$$

$$\frac{\sin\left(\dfrac{A-B}{2}\right)}{\sin\left(\dfrac{A+B}{2}\right)} = \frac{\tan\left(\dfrac{a-b}{2}\right)}{\cot\left(\dfrac{c}{2}\right)} \qquad \frac{\cos\left(\dfrac{A-B}{2}\right)}{\cos\left(\dfrac{A+B}{2}\right)} = \frac{\tan\left(\dfrac{a+b}{2}\right)}{\cot\left(\dfrac{c}{2}\right)}.$$

In the manuscript that he left before he died, Napier stated only one of these identities. Briggs added the other three in the remarks that he included as he helped to prepare the book for publication. Given the ease with which one can derive the three additional formulas, mathematicians generally credit Napier as the inventor of the complete set of four identities. The formulas enable one to determine all the measurements in a spherical triangle if four parts are known.

In *Descriptio*, Napier proposed a mnemonic system to aid in the memorization of a set of trigonometric formulas used for solving right triangles drawn on the surface of a sphere. Known as Napier's rule of circular parts, the method involved arranging in a circular pattern the values corresponding to the measurements of five parts of the triangle. The sine of any one part could then be conveniently determined from the cosines or tangents of the remaining parts.

Conclusion

Napier, who died on April 4, 1617, had a profound impact on mathematics through his invention of the concept of logarithms. The introduction of logarithms, the first significant mathematical idea to originate in Great Britain, established mathematics as a serious computational science. Ideas as significant as logarithms have seldom been introduced by a single individual working in isolation without building on foundational ideas introduced by earlier mathematicians. Napier's claim in the introduction to *Descriptio* that the reader would find that this small book gave as much as a thousand big books was not much of an exaggeration. In the late 18th century, French mathematician Pierre-Simon de Laplace commented that logarithms doubled the life of an astronomer by shortening the time needed to be spent on computations. With the invention of slide rules and the creation of extensive tables of values, logarithms immediately became and remained the primary method of computing products, quotients, and roots for the next 350 years. Logarithmic scales continue to be used in scientific applications, including the pH scale to measure the acidity of liquids; the decibel scale to quantify the intensity of sound; and the Richter scale to determine the power of an earthquake.

FURTHER READING

Baron, Margaret E. "Napier, John." In *Dictionary of Scientific Biography*, vol. 9, edited by Charles C. Gillispie, 609–613. New York: Scribner, 1972. Encyclopedic biography including a detailed description of the basis for his logarithms.

Boyer, Carl, and Uta Merzbach. *A History of Mathematics.* 2nd ed. New York: Wiley, 1991. Chapter 16 relates Napier's work to that of his contemporaries.

Hodges, Jeremy. "Significant Scots: John Napier," Electric Scotland. com. Available online. URL: http://www.electricscotland.com/history/other/john_napier.htm. Accessed April 18, 2005. Online reprint of Hodges's extensive July 8, 2000, article from the *Daily Mail.*

MathPages.com. "The Secret Confidence of Nature: 8.1, Kepler, Napier, and the Third Law," under "Reflections on Relativity." Available online. URL: http://www.mathpages.com/rr/s8-01/8-01.html. Accessed May 20, 2005. This article explains Johannes Kepler's indebtedness to Napier for his invention of logarithms as well as Napier's connections to King James I, Tycho Brahe, and William Shakespeare.

O'Connor, J. J., and E. F. Robertson. "John Napier," MacTutor History of Mathematics Archive, University of Saint Andrews.

Available online. URL: http://www-groups.dcs.st-andrews. ac.uk/~history/Mathematicians/Napier.html. Accessed May 25, 2005. Online biography, from the University of Saint Andrews, Scotland.

Reimer, Luetta, and Wilbert Reimer. "Magician or Mathematician?: John Napier." In *Mathematicians Are People, Too: Stories from the Lives of Great Mathematicians*, 36–43. Parsippany, N.J.: Seymour, 1990. Life story with historical facts and fictionalized dialogue; intended for elementary school students.

4

Pierre de Fermat

(1601–1665)

Pierre de Fermat investigated properties of prime numbers, divisibility, and
powers of integers that established the
discipline of modern number theory.
*(University of Rochester, courtesy of
AIP Emilio Segrè Visual Archives)*

Father of Modern Number Theory

Through the hundreds of letters that he sent to other mathematicians, Pierre de Fermat (pronounced fair-MAH or FER-mat) contributed influential ideas to four areas of mathematics. With René
Descartes, he shares the credit for developing the basic ideas of analytic geometry. He discovered techniques for finding maximums,
minimums, tangents, and areas of simple curves that foreshadowed
the introduction of calculus. Through his correspondence with
Blaise Pascal, he helped to formulate the fundamental ideas of the

theory of probability. His theorems and conjectures about prime numbers, divisibility, and powers of integers led to the development of modern number theory.

Professional Life Leaves Time for Mathematical Investigations

Pierre de Fermat was born in August 1601 at Beaumont-de-Lomagne in southern France. Records of the local Catholic church indicate that he was baptized on August 20 of that year, although he may have been born three days earlier on August 17. Dominique Fermat, his father, was a prosperous leather merchant who served as second consul of the town, a position similar to that of a mayor. Claire de Long, his mother, came from a prominent family that had acquired the social rank of *noblesse de robe* through their judicial service as members of the *parlement* (court system).

After studying classical languages and literature at a local Franciscan school and attending the University of Toulouse, Fermat earned the degree Bachelor of Civil Laws from the University of Orléans in May 1631. Two months later, he married Louise de Long, his mother's cousin, with whom he had two sons and three daughters. He purchased the offices of *conseiller* (counselor) in the court at Toulouse and *commissaire aux requêtes* (commissioner of requests) in Palais. Holding these positions in the judicial system entitled Fermat to add the particle *de* to his name as an indicator of his social rank. The deaths of a number of senior court officials allowed him to advance in his profession to the office of *conseiller aux enquêtes* (counselor of inquiries) in 1638, to the criminal court and the Grand Chamber in 1642, and to a position on the king's council in 1648.

Fermat's positions in the judicial system afforded him ample time to pursue other interests. Fluent in five languages, he wrote essays about Latin and Greek philology and enjoyed writing poetry in Latin, French, and Spanish. His greatest devotion was to the study of mathematics, a passionate interest that consumed most of his personal time from the late 1620s until his death on January 12, 1665. He communicated his many mathematical discoveries in letters to a large circle of professional mathematicians. Despite encouragement from several colleagues, he refused to allow his work to be published, did not formally record the logical progression of most of his ideas, and usually declined to share the proofs of his theorems. The mathematicians with whom he corresponded incorporated many of his ideas into their published works on analytic geometry, probability, and calculus. His deep investigations into number theory remained largely unappreciated until a century later, when Swiss mathematician Leonhard Euler and his contemporaries discovered the richness of his work.

Origins of Analytic Geometry

In the 1620s before beginning his legal studies at Orléans, Fermat spent several years in Bordeaux studying with a group of mathematicians who were editing and publishing the algebraic works of the 16th-century French mathematician François Viète. At the same time, Fermat was also attempting to reconstruct the classic geometrical work *Plane Loci*, written in the third century B.C.E. by the Greek mathematician Apollonius of Perga. Fermat used Viète's new methods of algebra to try to reproduce the reasoning that led Apollonius to discover his results about collections of points that form lines and circles. By introducing a system of coordinates based on a horizontal line called an axis and a moving line that met the axis at some fixed angle, Fermat found that he could create equations involving two variables to describe the locus of points on any given line or circle. For these two simple types of curves, he had discovered a method linking algebraic equations to geometric shapes.

After finishing his reconstruction of Apollonius's work, Fermat spent two years developing a more general theory of equations and graphs that he explained in a manuscript titled *Ad locos planos et solidos isagoge* (Introduction to plane and solid loci). In this treatise, he explained that every equation of the form $ax^2 + by^2 + cxy + dx + ey + f = 0$ described a line, a circle, a parabola, a hyperbola, or an ellipse. Retaining the geometrical concept that parabolas, ellipses, and hyperbolas were obtained by slicing a three-dimensional cone with a plane, he used the term *solid curves* to mean these three types of conic sections and reserved the term *plane curves* to mean lines and circles. By defining the systematic connection between the equations and the graphs of these basic functions,

Fermat laid the foundations of the branch of mathematics known as analytic geometry.

In 1636, Fermat sent his two unpublished manuscripts to Marin Mersenne, a Jesuit priest and French mathematician living in Paris who served the mathematical community by communicating new discoveries to a network of mathematicians throughout France. At the same time, another French mathematician, René Descartes, was finalizing a manuscript titled *Discours de la méthode pour bien conduire sa raison et chercher la vérité dans les sciences* (Discourse on the method for rightly directing one's reason and searching for truth in the sciences) and its mathematical appendix, *La géométrie* (The geometry). In his treatises, Descartes presented the same basic techniques relating algebra and geometry that Fermat had described. The primary difference between their approaches was that Fermat started with an algebraic equation and produced the corresponding curve, while Descartes proceeded from the geometric description of a curve to obtain its equation. The two mathematicians who developed their ideas independently share the credit for introducing this method of relating equations and graphs. Since Descartes's work addressed a more general collection of functions and received wider circulation after being published in 1637, mathematicians more closely associate his name with the discovery of analytic geometry and still refer to the system of x and y coordinates as "Cartesian" coordinates.

Fermat continued to develop and share his thoughts on analytic geometry during the next 15 years. After reading *La géométrie*, he criticized Descartes's classification of curves as being unnecessarily complicated, suggesting that curves of degrees $2n$ and $2n-1$ could be understood in terms of simpler curves of degree n. These comments initiated a bitter, lifelong dispute between the two mathematicians. In his 1643 memoir entitled *Isagoge ad locus ad superficiem* (Introduction to surface loci), Fermat attempted to generalize the methods of analytic geometry to analyze three-dimensional objects. Although his techniques did not constitute a workable mathematical approach, the ideas he suggested laid the algebraic foundation for a system of higher-dimensional analytic geometry. In his 1650 manuscript, *Novus secundarum et ulterioris ordinis radicum in analyticis usus* (New analytic uses for secondary and higher order roots), he noted that equations involving one, two, and three variables corresponded to points, curves, and surfaces, respectively. His idea of classifying an equation in terms of the number of variables and the corresponding dimension of the resulting locus of points represented another important conceptual development that enabled later mathematicians to generalize the basic theories that he and Descartes had created.

Essential Ideas in Calculus

As his ideas on analytic geometry matured, Fermat developed several techniques for analyzing the graphs of parabolas, hyperbolas, and spirals. Thirty years before Englishman Sir Isaac Newton and German Gottfried Leibniz discovered the branch of mathematics known as calculus, Fermat began applying many of the subject's central concepts to restricted classes of functions. In his initial letter to Mersenne in 1636, he described how he had generalized the results on spirals that had been obtained by the Greek mathematician Archimedes of Syracuse in the third century B.C.E. Modeling his approach on Archimedes' work with spirals of the form $r = a\theta$, he developed a method for finding areas related to spirals given by the more general equation $r = (a\theta)^n$ for any positive integer n. In this same letter, he also conveyed his ideas about the motion of freely falling bodies and gave two examples of a method that he had devised to find the maximum point on a parabola.

When Mersenne requested further details about his methods, Fermat sent him the manuscript *Methodus ad disquirendam maximam et minimam* (Method for determining maxima and minima). This work explained his techniques for finding the highest and lowest points on a curve, the points that in modern terminology are known as local extrema or local maximums and minimums. Borrowing the technique "adequality" from the third-century Greek mathematician Diophantus of Alexandria, he analyzed a given curve by assuming that the curve took its extreme value at two points A and $A + E$. After creating an equation that related these two roots to one of the coefficients in the equation of the curve, he set the two roots equal to each other. Solving the resulting equation produced the unique maximum or minimum point.

At the end of this manuscript, Fermat presented two applications of his method of maximums and minimums showing how to find the slope of the line that was tangent at any point on a parabola or hyperbola and how to find the center of gravity of a section of a parabola. When Descartes learned of Fermat's method of tangents in 1638, he criticized it as illogical and of limited use but changed his opinion when he realized that it was more efficient than the complicated method he had devised. Although Fermat limited his analysis to curves of the forms $y^m = kx^n$ and $x^n y^m = k$, where m and n are positive integers, his methods generalized to all functions and were consistent with the modern definition of derivative that is used to find the slope of a tangent line.

Fermat continued to develop additional calculus techniques during the next 25 years. In a letter to French mathematician Pierre Brûlard de Saint-Martin dated 1643, he described a method for classifying extreme values as maximums or minimums depending on the concavity of the curve at the point, a criterion now known as the second derivative test. By 1646, he had developed a method for finding areas under parabolas and hyperbolas of the forms $y^m = kx^n$ and $x^n y^m = k$ using the sum of an infinite collection of rectangles. Although he used a geometric series to determine the variable widths of the rectangles rather than using rectangles of a uniform width, his concept captured the essential ideas of the modern theory of integration. In 1660, he allowed French mathematician Antoine de La Loubère to publish his method for finding the arc length of a curve in an appendix to one of La Loubère's books. This appendix titled

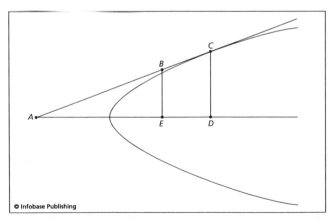

© Infobase Publishing

Fermat developed a method using the sides of similar triangles to find the slope of the line tangent to a parabola.

De linearum curvarum cum lineas rectis comparatione dissertation geometrica (Geometric dissertation on the comparison of curved lines with straight lines), listing the author cryptically as M. P. E. A. S., was the only formal publication of Fermat's work during his lifetime.

In 1662, Fermat used his theory of maximums to derive the law of optics known as Fermat's principle. The rule states that light rays seek the shortest path as they reflect and refract through mediums of different densities such as air and water. Although he had criticized Descartes's original statement of the principle in 1637, Fermat reconsidered his opinion, and in the manuscript *Analysis ad refractions* (Analysis of refractions), he provided the mathematical basis for the physical law. This application of calculus to a physical situation was one of his few ventures outside the realm of theoretical mathematics.

Fermat discovered all the central ideas of calculus, but mathematicians do not consider him to be one of the inventors of calculus. He did not realize that the slope of the tangent line and the area under a curve were functions of the given curve. He also missed the concept known as the fundamental theorem of calculus, which expresses the inverse relationship between derivatives and integrals. His informal manuscripts dealing with a restricted set of functions were not widely circulated and did not significantly impact the subsequent development of the more general ideas of calculus. However, Newton did credit Fermat's ideas on tangent lines for providing an inspiration for his definition of the derivative.

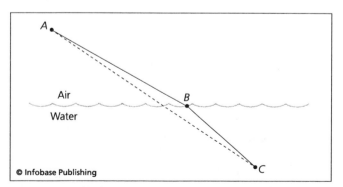

In optics, Fermat's principle explains that light rays traveling at different speeds through air and water follow a refracted path to minimize the total time required to reach from point A to point B.

Fundamentals of the Theory of Probability

In 1654, French mathematician Blaise Pascal wrote to Fermat seeking his opinion about a fair way to resolve a wager in a game of dice. The letter described the situation of a gambler who was attempting to throw a six in eight tosses of a die when the game was interrupted after three unsuccessful attempts. Pascal asked how the gambler's wager and his potential winnings should be fairly divided in such an interrupted game. Fermat responded by calculating the number of possible outcomes that could have occurred in the game's remaining five tosses and the fraction of those outcomes in which the gambler would have successfully won his wager. Based on the ratio of these two numbers, he advised that the gambler should be reimbursed the appropriate fraction of the money.

During an intensive period lasting only six months, Pascal and Fermat exchanged a series of letters in which they formulated mathematical techniques for analyzing several games of chance. They outlined methods of calculation, offered critiques of each other's ideas, and gradually formulated the basic concepts of a theory of probability. In 1657, Dutch mathematician Christiaan Huygens included many of their ideas on gambling problems in his brief but sophisticated pamphlet *De ratiociniis in ludo aleae* (On reasoning in games of dice), which remained the primary text on probability theory until the end of the century. Much of Fermat and Pascal's joint work on mathematical expectation and counting techniques eventually appeared in 1713, when Swiss mathematician Jakob Bernoulli developed their techniques into the more formal theory of probability in his book *Ars conjectandi* (The art of conjecturing).

Questions about Primes and Divisibility Define Modern Number Theory

Fermat made his most significant contributions to the branch of mathematics known as number theory. Building on the work of Diophantus, Apollonius, and other Greek mathematicians, he refined the focus of the discipline and introduced new problems and results that ultimately transformed classical number theory into modern number theory. In contrast to his Greek predecessors who had studied both integers and fractions, Fermat restricted his attention exclusively to the properties of positive integers and to whole number solutions of equations with integer coefficients.

Through an exchange of letters with mathematical colleagues in Paris, Fermat communicated theorems that he claimed to have proven, conjectures that he considered plausible, examples that illustrated interesting ideas, and challenge problems that he hoped would generate interest in the subject. Contrary to his practice in other areas of mathematics, his writings on number theory included only one complete proof and gave very few hints of the methods he used to obtain his results. From 1643 to 1654, during a time of political turmoil and poor health, he completely isolated himself, ceasing all correspondence while he worked on this theory of numbers.

Fermat's earliest work in number theory dealt with relationships between a positive integer and the sum of its proper divisors—those smaller positive numbers that divide it. He discovered a formula that gave the sum of a number's proper divisors and used it to study perfect numbers—those that are equal to the sum of their proper divisors. He proved that there were no perfect numbers having 20 or 21 digits, contradicting a widely held belief that there were perfect numbers of every size. Generalizing the concept of perfect numbers, he extensively studied numbers such as 120 and 672, which were half the sum of their proper divisors, and found numbers that were a third, a fourth, and a fifth of the sum of their proper divisors. Investigating the related problem of friendly or amicable pairs of numbers, he determined that each of the numbers 17,296 and 18,416 was the sum of the other's proper divisors. Marin Mersenne, a Jesuit priest and mathematician living in Paris, published several of Fermat's results about proper divisors in his 1637 treatise *L'Harmonie Universelle* (Universal harmony).

Many of Fermat's number theory results dealt with prime numbers—integers such as 2, 3, 5, 7, 11, ... whose only proper divisor is the number 1. In a series of letters that he exchanged with Bernard Frenicle de Bessy, one of France's leading number theorists, he shared several new results about prime numbers of the form $2^n - 1$, numbers that eventually became known as Mersenne primes. Fermat proved that if n is not prime, then neither is $2^n - 1$. He proved that if n is prime, then all the divisors of $2^n - 1$ must be of the form $2mn + 1$, and he gave the example that $2 \cdot 3 \cdot 37 + 1 = 223$ is one of the divisors of $2^{37} - 1$. He also investigated the connections between Mersenne numbers and perfect numbers.

In a 1640 letter to Frenicle, Fermat stated the fundamental result now known as Fermat's theorem or Fermat's little theorem: if a is an integer and p is a prime number, then $a^p - a$ is divisible by p. This important result is not only central to the study of prime numbers but also an essential principle in group theory, equation theory, and other branches of modern mathematics. In a manner typical of Fermat, he wrote that his proof of this result was too long to include in the letter. Euler produced the first known proof of this result in 1736 and generalized the theorem in 1760. Since then, many other mathematicians have discovered additional significant properties related to this deep theorem.

Throughout his career, Fermat struggled with the question of whether or not all numbers of the form $2^{2^n} + 1$ are prime. The first five numbers of this form 3, 5, 17, 257, and 65,537 are prime, but in 1732, Euler discovered that the next number in this sequence, $2^{32} + 1 = 4,294,967,297$, is divisible by 641. In letters to Frenecle, Mersenne, and Pascal, Fermat wrote that he strongly believed that this conjecture was true and, at one time, claimed to have a proof. Although he was incorrect in his belief, the numbers of this form that are prime are known today as "Fermat primes" in his honor.

Writing Numbers as Sums of Powers

A significant portion of Fermat's work in number theory concerned questions about the sum of the powers of two numbers. In a letter to Mersenne written on Christmas Day 1640, he stated that every prime number of the form $4n + 1$ could be expressed as the sum of the squares of two integers in only one way and that no primes of the form $4n - 1$ could be expressed in that manner. Examples of primes that can be written as the sum of two squares are 37, which can be written as $4 \cdot 9 + 1$ and as $1^2 + 6^2$, and 73, which can be written as $4 \cdot 18 + 1$ and as $3^2 + 8^2$. In the following years, he used this important result many times to derive other properties of prime numbers and their powers, including the fact that every integer can be written as a sum of four squares.

The only complete proof of a number theoretic result that Fermat ever revealed concerned sums of powers of numbers. He proved that if a right triangle has sides of integer lengths a, b, and c, then its area cannot be a perfect square. In the form of equations, this theorem states that there cannot be four integers a, b, c, and d for which and $a^2 + b^2 = c^2$ and $\frac{1}{2}ab = d^2$. In the 1659 manuscript *Relation des nouvelles découvertes en la science des nombres* (Account of new discoveries in the science of numbers), which he asked his friend Pierre de Carcavi to forward to Huygens, Fermat provided a detailed proof of this theorem using the method of infinite descent that he had invented. He showed that if there was a right triangle satisfying the given equations, then he could create a smaller right triangle that also satisfied the necessary conditions. Since this process of finding smaller and smaller positive integers cannot continue indefinitely, he reasoned that there could not be a first such triangle. He then used this result to prove that the equation $x^4 + y^4 = z^4$ had no integer solutions.

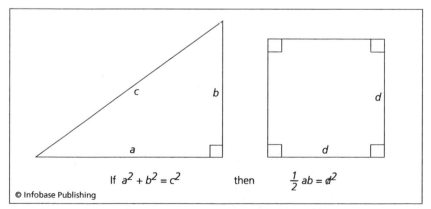

If $a^2 + b^2 = c^2$ then $\frac{1}{2}ab = d^2$

© Infobase Publishing

Using his method of infinite descent, Fermat proved that the area of a right triangle with integer sides could not be a perfect square. This result enabled him to prove Fermat's last theorem for the case $n = 4$.

In January 1657, Fermat tried to stimulate interest in number theory within the European mathematical community by issuing a public challenge that circulated under the title "Two mathematical problems posed as insoluble to French, English, Dutch and all mathematicians of Europe by Monsieur de Fermat, Councilor of the King in the Parlement of Toulouse." The first problem asked the participants to find a perfect cube that together with its proper divisors adds up to a perfect square. Fermat provided the example of 7, explaining that when $7^3 = 343$ is added to its proper divisors 1, 7, and 49, it produces the square number $400 = 20^2$. The second problem asked for a perfect square that when added to its proper divisors produces a perfect cube.

The challenge received no response because among the small percentage of mathematicians who were interested in number theory, very few knew the advanced techniques required to work on these problems. After only a month, Fermat revealed that, other than the example that he had provided and the obvious case of the number 1, neither equation had any solutions. In February 1657, he posed a third challenge problem, asking potential solvers to find all integer solutions of the equation $nx^2 + 1 = y^2$ for any fixed, non-square integer n. To provide direction to his colleagues, he presented the examples $3(1)^2 + 1 = (2)^2$ and $3(4)^2 + 1 = (7)^2$. English mathematician John Wallis and Irish mathematician William Brouncker submitted the only solution, obtaining the answer

$$x = \frac{2r}{n - r^2}, y = \frac{r^2 + n}{r^2 - n}$$ for any integer r by the method of contin-

ued fractions. When Fermat rejected their solution insisting that they restrict their attention to integer solutions, the two refused to continue corresponding with him.

Among all the theorems that Fermat claimed to have proven, the one that generated the most interest was "Fermat's last theorem." In the margin of his copy of Diophantus's *Arithmetica* (Arithmetic), Fermat wrote a note asserting that he had discovered a remarkable proof that the equation $x^n + y^n = z^n$ had no integer solutions when $n > 2$ but that the margin was too small to contain his proof. Mathematicians learned of this claim in 1670, five years after Fermat's death, when his son Clèment-Samuel published Fermat's annotations of Diophantus's book under the title *Observations sur*

Diophante (Observations on Diophantus). In 1659, Fermat had sent to Huygens a proof for the case $n = 4$ and had earlier challenged other mathematicians to prove the theorem for the case $n = 3$, but he left no general proof that addressed larger values of n.

After proving or disproving all the other claims and conjectures that Fermat had made in his notes, letters, and manuscripts, mathematicians had neither proved nor disproved Fermat's last theorem. By the end of the 18th century, Euler's 1738 proof for the case $n = 3$ represented the only progress they had made. Between 1825 and 1832, French-born mathematicians Adrien-Marie Legendre, Gabriel Lamé, and Lejeune Dirichlet created proofs for the cases $n = 5$, 7, and 14. By 1850, French mathematician Sophie Germain and German mathematician Ernst Kummer had each showed that the theorem held for large classes of prime exponents. Finally, in 1994, English mathematician Andrew Wiles completed the proof, showing that Fermat's last theorem is true whenever $n > 2$.

Conclusion

During the three-and-a-half centuries since Fermat's death, thousands of mathematicians have dedicated their efforts to proving or disproving Fermat's last theorem and the other claims and conjectures that he had stated without proof. In the course of their work, they accomplished what Fermat had hoped to achieve through his challenge problems and his voluminous correspondence—to initiate wide-ranging explorations into general properties of numbers and their related applications in other branches of mathematics. In addition to proving the theorems themselves, the efforts of these mathematicians have resulted in significant developments in the theory of complex numbers, algebraic geometry, elliptic function theory, cryptology, and other branches of mathematics and science as well as the maturation of modern number theory as a major discipline within the field of mathematics.

FURTHER READING

Bell, Eric T. *Men of Mathematics.* New York: Simon and Schuster, 1965. In this classic history of European mathematics from 1600 to 1900, chapter 4 is devoted to Fermat's life and work.

Boyer, Carl, and Uta Merzbach. *A History of Mathematics.* 2nd ed. New York: Wiley, 1991. Chapter 17 discusses Fermat's work and that of other 17th-century mathematicians.

Dunham, William. *The Mathematical Universe: An Alphabetical Journey through the Great Proofs, Problems, and Personalities.* New York: Wiley, 1994. Chapter F profiles Fermat's life and work.

Kleiner, Israel. "Fermat: The Founder of Modern Number Theory." *Mathematics Magazine* 78, no. 1 (2005): 3–14. Recent journal article about several of Fermat's number theoretic results that led to subsequent developments in mathematics.

Mahoney, Michael Sean. *The Mathematical Career of Pierre de Fermat, 1601–1665.* 2nd ed. Princeton, N.J.: Princeton University Press, 1973. Authoritative, full-length account of Fermat's life and mathematics.

———. "Fermat, Pierre de." In *Dictionary of Scientific Biography*, vol. 4, edited by Charles C. Gillispie, 566–576. New York: Scribner, 1972. Encyclopedic biography including a detailed description of his most important work.

O'Connor, J. J., and E. F. Robertson. "Pierre de Fermat," MacTutor History of Mathematics Archive, University of Saint Andrews. Available online. URL: http://www-groups.dcs.st-andrews. ac.uk/~history/Mathematicians/Fermat.html. Accessed June 10, 2005. Online biography, from the University of Saint Andrews, Scotland.

Blaise Pascal

(1623–1662)

Blaise Pascal invented a calculating machine, studied the arithmetic triangle that bears his name, and helped to establish the discipline of probability theory. *(Library of Congress)*

Coinventor of Probability Theory

As a mathematician, inventor, scientist, and writer, Blaise Pascal (pronounced pahs-KAHL) worked at the forefront of knowledge in multiple disciplines. He designed and built the first commercially available mechanical calculating machine. His experiments with barometers helped to establish hydrostatic principles related to air pressure and vacuums. His writings on religion, philosophy, and ethics met with critical acclaim in the literary world. Pascal's theorem introduced new ideas in projective geometry, and his work with cycloids introduced new techniques of integration. Through his analysis of Pascal's triangle and his correspondence with Pierre de Fermat, he helped to lay the foundations of probability theory.

Discoveries in Projective Geometry

Blaise Pascal was born on June 19, 1623, in Clermont-Ferrand in the Auvergne region of central France. Étienne Pascal, his father, was a lawyer from a wealthy family who maintained an active interest in current developments within the Parisian mathematical community. Antoinette Bégone, his mother, died when he was three, leaving his father to raise him and his two sisters, Gilberte and Jacqueline. Because Blaise suffered frequent health problems, his father, who home-educated the three children, decided not to introduce his son to mathematics and removed all his math books from the house.

In spite of these restrictions, Pascal initiated his own independent study of geometry at the age of 12. When he produced a proof that the three angles in a triangle add up to 180 degrees, his father recognized his mathematical talent and gave him a copy of Euclid's *Elements*, the classic mathematics book that had been written in the third century B.C.E by the Greek mathematician Euclid of Alexandria. Within two years, Pascal started to accompany his father to the weekly meetings of a circle of mathematicians and scientists at the Paris home of Jesuit priest Marin Mersenne. There he met French mathematician Gérard Desargues, who shared with the group his treatise *Brouillon project d'une atteinte aux événemens des rencontres du cône avec un plan* (Schematic sketch of what happens when a cone meets a plane), which introduced the new field of projective geometry.

In June 1639, at the age of 16, Pascal presented to the group a one-page document in which he outlined the principle of projective geometry known as Pascal's theorem. The result dealt with a hexagon inscribed in a conic section—the six-sided polygon formed by joining six points that lie on a circle, ellipse, parabola, or hyperbola. In projective geometry where an additional point at infinity is adjoined to the standard x-y plane, whenever any two sides of such a hexagon are extended indefinitely, the resulting lines meet in a

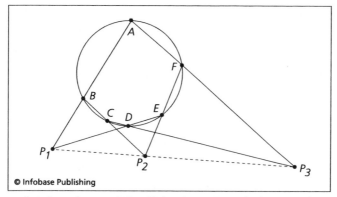

At the age of 16, Pascal proved that if the six vertices of a hexagon lie on a circle, a parabola, an ellipse, or a hyperbola, then the three points formed by the intersection of pairs of opposite sides will lie on a line known as the hexagon's Pascal line.

point. In his theorem, Pascal proved that the three points formed by the intersections of pairs of opposite sides of such a hexagon must lie on a straight line called the hexagon's Pascal line. He used the term *mystic hexagram* to describe the 60 different hexagons and their corresponding Pascal lines that could be created by considering all possible orderings of six points on a conic. Pascal's theorem remains a fundamental result that links hundreds of theorems from classical geometry to the projective geometry studied by mathematicians in the 19th century.

Pascal continued to develop his ideas on inscribed hexagons, and in February 1640, he published the pamphlet *Essai pour les coniques* (Essay on conics). This brief document presented several additional propositions related to Pascal's theorem and outlined his plan to develop a comprehensive study of conics in the projective plane. In subsequent years, he periodically worked on this project, producing a draft of several chapters in 1654, but never published the complete work. The first chapter of his unfinished manuscript on conics presented the basic ideas of projective geometry in a format that was more accessible than Desargues's *Brouillon project*. In another section of the incomplete treatise, he presented a thorough description of the mystic hexagram, Pascal's theorem, and their applications. The work also included solutions of problems from classical Greek geometry that demonstrated the effectiveness of projective geometry as an alternative to the competing geometry being developed by French mathematician René Descartes.

Calculating Machine Performs Addition and Subtraction

In 1640, Pascal's family moved to Rouen, where his father had accepted a governmental position as administrator of taxes. Observing the numerous arithmetical calculations involved in his father's work, he attempted to mechanize the process of computation. By the end of 1642, he had designed a machine that used the movement of gears to perform the operations of addition and subtraction. During the next three years, with encouragement from Pierre Séguier, the chancellor of France, he experimented with 50 different prototypes. In 1645, he finalized his design and formed a company to manufacture and sell his arithmetic machine, the Pascaline. Although German astronomer Wilhelm Schickard had invented a similar calculating machine in 1623, the Pascaline was the first mechanical calculator offered for commercial sale.

Pascal explained the operation of his machine in an 18-page pamphlet titled *Lettre dédicatoire à Monseigneur le Chancelier sur le sujet de la machine nouvellement inventée par le sieur B. P. pour faire toutes sortes d'opérations d'arithmétique par un movement réglé sans plume ni jetons avec un avis nécessaire à ceux qui auront curiosité de voir ladite machine et de s'en servir* (Letter of dedication to my lord the chancellor on the subject of the machine newly invented by Mister B. P. to perform all sorts of operations of arithmetic by a regulated movement without pen or counters with necessary advice for those who will have the curiosity to see the machine and to try it). In addition to explaining the device's purpose, abilities, and construction, the pamphlet acknowledged his indebtedness to Chancellor Séguier and invited prospective customers to view and purchase the machine at the home of mathematician Gilles de Roberval. In 1649, Pascal obtained a monopoly by royal decree for the exclusive manufacture and sale of his calculating device. In 1652, he demonstrated his machine for Queen Christina of Sweden and presented her with one as a gift. Although the calculator's capabilities generated great interest among mathematicians,

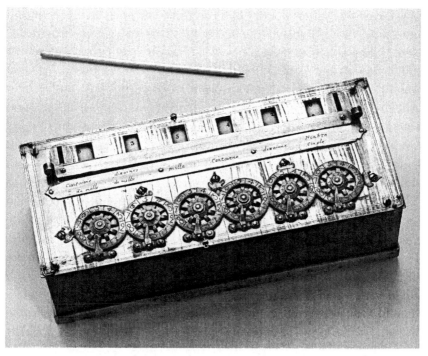

Pascal invented the first mechanical calculating machine to be sold commercially. Known as the Pascaline, the machine used an array of gears to add and subtract numbers, producing answers of up to six digits. *(The Image Works)*

scientists, businessmen, and wealthy individuals, its high price limited its commercial success.

Experiments on Vacuums and Air Pressure

From 1646 to 1654, Pascal worked with a group of scientists to design and perform experiments on barometric pressure and vacuums. In the late 1630s and early 1640s, Italian scientists Galileo Galilei and Evangelista Torricelli had performed experiments using tubes filled with various liquids in their attempts to establish the existence of the vacuum, a controversial concept that had not been scientifically demonstrated. Between October 1646 and February 1647, Pascal and his father replicated some of Torricelli's work and carried out several variations of their own using water and wine in custom-made tubes as long as 40 feet attached to the masts of sailing ships. In his October 1647 report on these experiments, entitled *Expériences nouvelles touchant le vide* (New experiments concerning the vacuum), he cautiously concluded that his work pointed toward the existence of an apparent vacuum.

In September 1648, he designed an experiment to measure the air pressure at different altitudes. His brother-in-law, Florin Périer, conducted the simultaneous experiment at Clermont-Ferrand and at the higher elevation on the summit of Puy de Dôme. The experiment demonstrated that air pressure decreased as elevation above sea level increased. Pascal produced a 20-page report on this experiment titled *Récit de la grande expérience de l'équilibre des liqueurs projetée par le sieur B. P. pour l'accomplissement du traité qu'il a promis dans son abrégé touchant le vide et faite par le sieur F. P. en une des plus hautes montagnes d'Auvergne* (Report of the great experiment of equilibrium of liquids planned by Mister B. P. for the completion of a treatise that he promised in his abridged report concerning the vacuum and performed by Mister F. P. on one of the highest mountains in Auvergne). In this report, he claimed that his research gave scientific evidence for the existence of the vacuum and for the weight of the air confirming the theories proposed by Descartes, Mersenne, and other scientists.

After conducting several years of additional experiments and revising his theories based on the results they produced, Pascal wrote *Traités de l'équilibre des liqueurs et de la pesanteur de la masse de l'air. Contenant l'explication des causes de divers effets de la nature qui n'avaient point été bien connus jusques ici, et particulièrement*

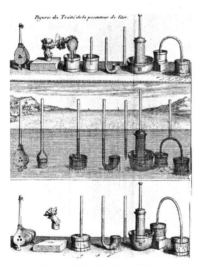

Pascal's *Traités de l'équilibre des liqueurs et de la pesanteur de la masse de l'air* (Treatises on the equilibrium of liquids and on the weight of the mass of the air) discussed the principle of the vacuum and the scientific theory of air pressure. *(Library of Congress)*

de ceux que l'on avait attribués à l'horreur du vide (Treatises on the equilibrium of liquids and on the weight of the mass of the air. Containing the explanation of the causes of diverse effects of nature that have not been well-understood until this point, and particularly to those who have ascribed to the horror of the vacuum). In this work, Pascal explained in detail the laws of hydrostatics and described the effects of air pressure. He included a summary of the work of Galileo, Torricelli, and others, along with his own contributions, to provide a comprehensive treatment of both the history and the current state of this branch of physics. He offered rigorous scientific procedures and explanations to refute the theory known as the "horror of the vacuum," which denied the existence of the vacuum on religious grounds. Although this 1654 treatise was not published until 1663, by which time Irish chemist Robert Boyle and others had achieved further advances in the hydrostatics, Pascal's experiments and earlier writings contributed to the growing understanding of the principle of the vacuum and enabled other scientists to further develop the scientific theory of air pressure.

Foundations of Probability Theory and the Arithmetic Triangle

In 1654, Pascal turned his attention back to mathematics when Antoine Gombaud, chevalier de Méré, asked his advice on several questions about gambling. One inquiry asked how the money being wagered should be divided between two equally skilled players if the game was interrupted before either of them won. Another concerned the likelihood of throwing a particular number in a game of dice. Pascal posed the questions to French mathematician Pierre de Fermat. Through their correspondence during the next six months, the two formulated mathematical techniques for analyzing these and other games of chance. They outlined methods of calculation, offered critiques of each other's ideas, and gradually formulated the basic concepts of a theory of probability.

In this joint effort, Pascal focused his analysis on the determination of the number of possible outcomes in a specified game of chance. He became particularly interested in an arrangement of positive integers that he called the arithmetic triangle. Consisting of a collection of horizontal rows and vertical columns that he called parallel ranks and perpendicular ranks, respectively, each entry other than the border of ones was the sum of the number above it and the number to its left. This triangular arrangement of numbers had appeared in the writings of the 13th-century Iranian mathematician Nasīr al-Dīn al-Tūsī, the 14th-century Chinese mathematician Chu Shih-chieh, and several European mathematicians of the 16th and 17th centuries. Pascal discovered so many new patterns and relationships among the entries of the triangle that earlier mathematicians had not identified that the triangle is now known as Pascal's triangle.

In the 1654 work *Traité du triangle arithmétique, avec quelques petits traités sur la même matière* (Treatise on the arithmetic triangle, with several small treatises on the same matter), Pascal explained the construction of the triangle and its many properties. He noted, as earlier mathematicians had done, that the entries on the nth "base," or diagonal, add up to 2^n and form the binomial coefficients that, in modern notation, are written as $\binom{n}{0}, \binom{n}{1}, \binom{n}{2}, ... \binom{n}{n}$.

1	1	1	1	1	1	1	1	1	1
1	2	3	4	5	6	7	8	9	
1	3	6	10	15	21	28	36		
1	4	10	20	35	56	84			
1	5	15	35	70	126				
1	6	21	56	126					
1	7	28	84						
1	8	36							
1	9								
1									

Parallel ranks

Perpendicular ranks

© Infobase Publishing

Pascal investigated numerical relationships between the numbers arranged in parallel and perpendicular ranks in the arithmetic triangle that became known as Pascal's triangle.

Pascal also discovered new identities such as

$$\binom{n}{k} \div \binom{n}{k-1} = \frac{n+1-k}{k} \quad \text{and} \quad \binom{n}{k} \div \binom{n-1}{k-1} = \frac{n}{k} \quad \text{as well as}$$

a complicated formula that related binomial coefficients and sums of powers of positive integers. Summing the appropriate entries in the arithmetic triangle, he provided exact numerical probabilities for various situations in the relevant games of chance. In the final section of the treatise, he used the technique of mathematical induction to prove that the formulas he derived applied to numbers of all magnitudes. The circulation of Pascal's treatise popularized this seldom-used proof technique that Italian mathematician Francisco Maurolico had introduced in the 16th century.

Although Pascal never used the word *probability*, his work on the arithmetic triangle and his correspondence with Fermat laid the foundation for the modern theory of probability. His comprehensive and rigorous treatise on the arithmetic triangle formed the first systematic and rigorous study linked to many questions of arithmetic and combinatorial analysis. The modern branches of mathematics known as game theory and decision theory trace their roots to this work. Dutch mathematician Christiaan Huygens included many of Pascal's and Fermat's ideas on gambling problems in his 1657 pamphlet, *De ratiociniis in ludo aleae* (On reasoning in games of dice), which was the principal work on probability theory until the end of the century. Swiss mathematician Jakob Bernoulli developed their ideas on mathematical expectation and counting techniques into the more formal theory of probability in his 1713 book, *Ars conjectandi* (The art of conjecturing).

Study of the Cycloid Reinvigorates Pascal's Interest in Mathematics

In November 1654, after narrowly escaping death in a carriage accident, Pascal experienced a religious conversion. Abandoning his mathematical and scientific work, he dedicated his life to meditation and issues of religion, philosophy, and morality. To defend his friend Antoine Arnauld who had been charged with heresy for his controversial religious teachings, Pascal composed *Lettres écrites par*

Louis de Montalte à un provincial de ses amis (Letters written by Louis de Montalte to a provincial by his friends). This set of 18 essays published in 1657 under the fictitious name Louis de Montalte demonstrated his ability to make persuasive arguments in elegant prose. Pascal also wrote several reflections sharing his personal thoughts on human suffering, faith in God, morality, ethics, and philosophy but did not publish them during his lifetime.

After a four-year absence, Pascal resumed his mathematical research in 1658. When he successfully distracted himself from the pain of a toothache by thinking about a geometric curve, he interpreted the disappearance of his pain as a sign that he should return to the study of mathematics. The curve that occupied his thoughts, known as the cycloid or the *roulette*, is the path traced by a point on a circle as the circle rolls along a straight line. Applying the method of indivisibles that Italian mathematician Bonaventura Cavalieri had recently introduced, Pascal developed techniques to solve several geometrical problems related to segments of cycloids. Using these primitive techniques of integration, he was able to determine the area of any segment of the cycloid and the center of gravity of any segment. He also discovered how to determine the surface area, the volume, and the center of gravity of the solid formed by rotating the cycloid about the x-axis.

Writing under the name Amos Dettonville, Pascal issued a challenge to all mathematicians in France and England to solve a set of problems involving areas, volumes, and centers of gravity related to the cycloid. His friend the duke of Roannez offered a monetary prize for the best solution, and Roberval agreed to serve as the judge for the competition. After receiving two incorrect solutions and several letters from other mathematicians communicating related results, Pascal claimed the prize himself. In February 1659, he published four pamphlets collectively titled *Lettres de A. Dettonville contenant quelques-unes de ses inventions de géométrie* (Letters from A. Dettonville containing some of his inventions in geometry). Pascal wrote the various pieces in incremen-

The cycloid, or *roulette,* is the path traced by a point on a circle as the circle rolls along a straight line. In 1658, Pascal challenged other mathematicians to solve three problems relating to the area, volume, and center of gravity of objects related to the cycloid.

tal steps throughout the seven-month contest, as the correspondence he received from other mathematicians enabled him to develop more effective techniques. In addition to providing his solutions to the challenge problems and a description of his methods for working with cycloids, this 120-page collection explained techniques for dealing with spirals, parabolas, ellipses, triangular cylinders, and cones.

The widely circulated *Lettres* and the materials Pascal issued during the contest were both controversial and progressive. The summary of mathematical discoveries related to the cycloid that he published in the October 1658 pamphlet *Histoire de la roulette* (History of the roulette) omitted the contributions of several prominent mathematicians, raising charges of nationalism and bias. In several of the manuscripts that he included in *Lettres,* he introduced the new technique of integration by parts using objects he called trilines, onglets, and adjoints. German mathematician Gottfried Leibniz, one of the coinventors of calculus, credited Pascal's introduction of the characteristic triangle and other ideas contained in one of these manuscripts, *Traité des sinus du quart de cercle* (Treatise on the sines of a quadrant of a circle), for helping him to realize the connection between areas under curves and tangents to those curves.

After the conclusion of the cycloid contest, Pascal's health deteriorated as his lifelong battle with acute dyspepsia and chronic insomnia intensified. Abandoning most of his intellectual endeavors, he devoted the last years of his life to prayer and works of charity. In June 1662, he invited a poor, homeless family to share his house. When several of his houseguests became ill with smallpox, he moved to his sister, Gilberte Périer's, home. Two month's later on August 19, 1662, he died of cancer at the age of 39. While sorting through his possessions after his death, his sister discovered drawers and boxes filled with hundreds of slips of paper, some of which were threaded together sequentially on a piece of string. She collected these thoughts and his more lengthy writings on philosophy, ethics, and religion and published them in 1669 as the highly acclaimed literary work *Pensées* (Thoughts).

Conclusion

Pascal's talents allowed him to participate at the frontiers of several disciplines as an equal with other scholars who had deeper formal training and lengthier experience. If he had not moved so often between projects, he might have made greater contributions to civilization in general and to mathematics in particular. After discovering Pascal's theorem and inventing a mechanical calculating device, he conducted experiments on air pressure, investigated Pascal's triangle, wrote philosophical and religious treatises, and discovered new methods of integration with cycloids. Among these various achievements, his most significant contribution to mathematics was his establishment with Fermat of the fundamentals of the theory of probability.

FURTHER READING

Bell, Eric T. "Greatness and Misery of Man." In *Men of Mathematics*, 73–89. New York: Simon and Schuster, 1965. Chapter 5 presents an informative yet opinionated biography and evaluation of his mathematical work.

Coolidge, Julian L. "Blaise Pascal." In *The Mathematics of Great Amateurs*, 89–102. London: Oxford University Press, 1950. Discusses seven of Pascal's mathematical achievements.

Muir, Jane. "Blaise Pascal, 1623–1662." In *Of Men and Numbers: The Story of the Great Mathematicians*, 77–104. New York: Dover, 1996. Biographical sketch with a discussion of his mathematics.

O'Connor, J. J., and E. F. Robertson. "Blaise Pascal," MacTutor History of Mathematics Archive, University of Saint Andrews. Available online. URL: http://www-groups.dcs.st-andrews.ac.uk/~history/Mathematicians/Pascal.html. Accessed January 27, 2003. Online biography, from the University of Saint Andrews, Scotland.

Reimer, Luetta, and Wilbert Reimer. "Count on Pascal: Blaise Pascal." In *Mathematicians Are People, Too: Stories from the Lives of Great Mathematicians*, 52–61. Parsippany, N.J.: Seymour, 1990. Life story with historical facts and fictionalized dialogue; intended for elementary school students.

Taton, René. "Pascal, Blaise." In *Dictionary of Scientific Biography*, vol. 10, edited by Charles C. Gillispie, 330–342. New York: Scribner, 1972. Encyclopedic biography including a detailed description of his mathematical writings.

Sir Isaac Newton

(1642–1727)

Sir Isaac Newton proposed the first general theory of calculus and established the mathematical basis for the universal principle of gravitation. *(Library of Congress)*

Calculus, Optics, and Gravity

Sir Isaac Newton made significant discoveries in mathematics, optics, and physics that set the course for a century of further research in all three disciplines. His method of fluxions unified the work of prior mathematicians and established a general theory of calculus. Through experiments with prisms, lenses, and reflecting telescopes, he established new principles in optics and the theory of light. He formulated three laws of motion and proved the universal principle of gravitation. His insistence on experimental and mathematical bases for scientific theories changed the nature of scientific investigation.

Education and Early Life

Isaac Newton was born at Woolsthorpe Manor on his family's farm near Grantham in the county of Lincolnshire, England. By the calendar in use at the time, the date of his birth was December 25, 1642. This date corresponds to January 4, 1643, in the current Gregorian calendar that most European countries started using in 1581 but England did not adopt until 1752. His father, Isaac, an uneducated but prosperous farmer, died a few months before his son's birth. When Newton was three years old, his mother, Hannah Ayscough, moved to North Witham with her new husband, Reverend Barnabas Smith, leaving her son in the care of his maternal grandparents, James and Margery Ayscough.

A solitary child, Newton occupied his time drawing architectural sketches and constructing models, including a mouse-powered windmill and a four-wheeled cart propelled by a crank. At the age of 12, after attending two local day schools, he enrolled at the King's School in Grantham, where he showed occasional signs of academic promise. When his stepfather died in 1656, Newton's widowed mother returned to Woolsthorpe with a son and two daughters by her second marriage and withdrew Isaac from school to manage the family farm, a task for which he demonstrated no aptitude or interest. In 1660, he returned to the school, where he lived with the headmaster John Stokes while completing his final year of studies.

In June 1661, Newton entered Trinity College at Cambridge University. Although he intended to pursue a law degree, he developed stronger interests in philosophy, science, and mathematics. In several notebooks, including one that he titled *Quaestiones quaedam philosophicae* (Certain philosophical questions), he recorded his thoughts concerning influential books that he read, as well as his original ideas in all three disciplines. He was elected a scholar in 1664, a designation that provided him a four-year period of financial support toward a master's degree. In April 1665, he completed his undergraduate coursework and received his bachelor's degree.

Due to an outbreak of the plague in June 1665, the university closed for 18 months. Newton spent this intensive, creative time primarily in seclusion at Woolsthorpe developing ideas on mathematics and physics that led to his three greatest discoveries—the invention of calculus and his theories of light and gravitation. In the spring of 1666, he visited the university to use the mathematics library and to conduct some experiments on light rays, but most of his groundbreaking work during this period took place at the family farm.

When Cambridge University reopened in 1667, Newton returned to pursue further studies. He became a fellow of Trinity College, an honor that provided him with an annual stipend of approximately £60, with the provisions that he stay at the university, remain unmarried, and eventually enter the ministry. He completed his master's degree in 1668, and when Isaac Barrow retired the following year to become chaplain to the king, Newton succeeded him as the second Lucasian professor of mathematics at Cambridge University. This appointment provided an additional income of £100 per year, required him to deliver at least one weekly lecture throughout the school term, and obligated him to submit at least 10 of those lectures to the university's library each year. Although his lectures were often poorly attended (at times he spoke for 15 minutes to an empty lecture hall), he faithfully deposited manuscripts on optics, algebra, number theory, mechanics, and gravity during the first 16 years of his professorship. He held both the fellowship and the Lucasian chair for 32 years and managed to circumvent the ministerial requirement.

Infinite Series and the General Binomial Theorem

Newton made his first significant mathematical discoveries in the winter of 1664–65 during his final year of undergraduate study at Cambridge University. In 1656, English mathematician John Wallis had publicized his new method for finding areas under curves of the form $y = (1 - x^2)^n$ from $x = 0$ to $x = 1$ for positive integer values of n. Extending this procedure to apply to areas from $x = 0$ to an arbitrary value of x, Newton recognized that the coefficients of the resulting polynomials were the entries in the rows of the arithmetic triangle studied by French mathematician Blaise Pascal. Newton defined these binomial coefficients more generally as

$$\binom{n}{k} = \frac{n(n-1)(n-2)\cdots(n-k+1)}{k(k-1)(k-2)\cdots 1}$$ for any rational number n and

any positive integer k. This generalization enabled him to express the area under the curve $y = (1 - x^2)^n$ for any rational number n as an infinite sum of terms of the form

$$x - \binom{n}{1}\frac{x^3}{3} + \binom{n}{2}\frac{x^5}{5} - \binom{n}{3}\frac{x^7}{7} + \cdots .$$

These infinite sums, now called power series, provided the necessary foundation for the development of several other mathematical concepts. Newton produced power series for the trigonometric functions $\sin(x)$ and $\cos(x)$, their inverses $\arcsin(x)$ and $\arccos(x)$, the square root function $\sqrt{1-x}$, and the natural logarithmic function $\ln(1 + x)$. Using this last power series, Newton calculated

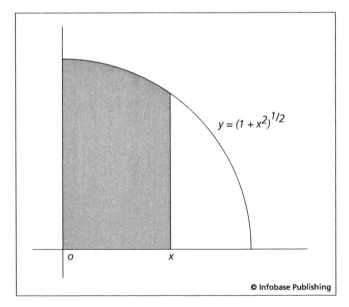

$$y = (1 + x^2)^{1/2}$$

O   x

By studying the polynomials corresponding to the areas under the curves $y = (1 - x^2)^n$, Newton discovered power series and the general binomial theorem.

logarithms of numbers that were accurate to more than 50 decimal places. His work with power series also enabled him to derive the general binomial theorem

$$(a + b)^n = a^n + \binom{n}{1} a^{n-1}b + \binom{n}{2} a^{n-2}b^2 + \binom{n}{3} a^{n-3}b^3 + \cdots.$$ For

positive integer values of n, the sum had only $n+1$ terms and agreed with the formula that was well known at the time. For fractional or negative values of n, the sum produced infinite series that he used to estimate the value of π to 16 decimal places and the values of square roots and cube roots of numbers to any desired degree of accuracy. Newton described his work with infinite series and the binomial theorem in a manuscript that he wrote in 1669 titled *De analysi per aequationes numero terminorum infinitas* (Of analysis by equations with an infinite number of terms). Barrow circulated the manuscript to several other mathematicians who were impressed by Newton's innovative ideas, but the full treatise remained unpublished until 1711.

Method of Fluxions Introduces the Formal Theory of Calculus

While the university was closed during the plague years of 1665–66, Newton made his most important mathematical discovery—the method of fluxions now known as calculus. Having spent much of his time at Cambridge reading both classical and current books on mathematics, he was familiar with the most recent work on areas, tangents, maxima and minima, arc lengths, volumes, and centers of gravity being done in France by René Descartes, Pierre de Fermat, Gilles de Roberval, and Pascal; in England by Barrow and John Wallis; in Italy by Bonaventura Cavalieri and Evangelista Torricelli; in the Netherlands by Johan Hudde; and in Belgium by Christiaan Huygens. Newton synthesized their various techniques with his own ideas to construct a comprehensive theory of calculus that he called the method of fluxions.

In 1664, Newton experimented with the concept of a difference quotient $\dfrac{f(x + o) - f(x)}{o}$ and an indefinitely small element denoted by o that he equated to zero in the final step of his calculations. This concept allowed him to determine mechanically many rules for derivatives of algebraic functions—functions that are products and powers of polynomials. During the following year, he modified his ideas to introduce the more general concept of a "fluxion" representing the speed of a continuously moving object. Envisioning all curves in two and three dimensions as the paths of moving objects whose x-, y-, and z-coordinates were functions of time, he let their fluxions represent the rates at which these "fluents" were changing. Initially, he used the letters p, q, and r to signify the fluxions corresponding to x, y, and z, respectively. He soon modified his notation and terminology, letting the "moment" $\dot{x}o$ represent the amount of change experienced by the quantity x during the passage of the infinitely small portion of time o.

Newton recorded his ideas about fluxions in an untitled set of notes that he wrote in October 1666. He provided a more detailed account in the 1669 manuscript *De analysi* and gave the first full demonstration of his calculus in the 1671 treatise *Methodus fluxionum et serierum infinitarum* (*Method of Fluxions and Infinite Series*). He repeatedly tried to arrange for the printing and distribution of the longer treatise, but booksellers were reluctant to publish highly mathematical works after Barrow's latest book failed to sell and bankrupted its printer. *Methodus* did not appear in print until 1736, when English mathematician John Colson translated it into English. The lack of good notation and the delay in the publication of his work contributed to the European mathematical community's slowness to embrace his revolutionary theory of calculus.

These early manuscripts on fluxions prominently featured the central idea that Newton recognized and that other mathematicians had missed—the inverse relationship between the operations of differentiation and integration that is known as the fundamental theorem of calculus. The first lines of *De analysi* presented the power rule for integrals explaining why the area under the curve $y = ax^{m/n}$ was given by the fluent $\dfrac{an}{m + n} x^{m+n/n}$. Later in the same

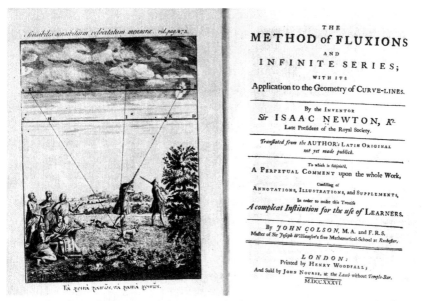

Newton explained his general theory of calculus in the 1671 treatise *Methodus fluxionum et serierum infinitarum* (Method of fluxions and infinite series). This illustration to a 1736 version depicts a hunter shooting at birds in flight with lines indicating how calculus makes analysis of movement possible. *(Library of Congress)*

manuscript, he used the binomial theorem to prove that the fluxion of this new function was the equation of the original curve. In *Methodus*, the first problem Newton solved was to calculate a fluxion using the technique now known as implicit differentiation. In the subsequent problem, he reversed the process integrating each term to recover the original equation. In both manuscripts, Newton explicitly mentioned the inverse nature of the two fundamental operations of calculus.

The array of techniques that Newton presented in *De analysi* and *Methodus* demonstrated the comprehensive nature of his theory of calculus. He used the power rules for derivatives and integrals of polynomial-type functions, the linearity properties that allow one to differentiate and integrate term by term, the method of implicit differentiation, and the product rule for derivatives as well as techniques for creating partial and higher-order derivatives. He explained several methods for finding the fluent corresponding to a given fluxion and produced a table of integrals for a selection of algebraic functions. Using infinite series, he showed how to obtain numerical results for fluxions and areas of nonalgebraic functions such as $\sin(x)$, $\cos(x)$, and $\ln(x)$.

In addition to explaining these mechanical processes of calculus, Newton showed how to apply them to the solution of various problems. To find the maximum and minimum points on a curve, he set its fluxion equal to zero and solved the resulting equation. He demonstrated how to create the tangent line to a curve at any point by taking the fluxion and evaluating it at that point. His method for determining the curvature of a function using the second derivative is equivalent to the modern technique. He introduced an iterative algorithm now known as Newton's method to approximate roots of equations using slopes of tangent lines. Applications involving distance, velocity, and acceleration appeared throughout both treatises. In *Methodus*, he introduced the concept of polar coordinates to calculate fluxions and areas associated with spirals.

Before Newton's manuscripts on fluxions were published, German mathematician Gottfried Leibniz independently developed an equivalent, comprehensive theory of calculus. He announced his methods in the paper *Nova methodus pro maximis et minimis, itemque tangentibus, quae nec fractus nec irrationales quantitates moratur, et singulare pro illis calculi genus* (A new method for maxima and minima, as well as tangents, which is obstructed neither by fractional nor

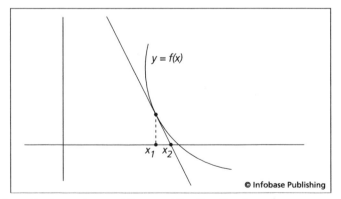

Newton's method uses tangent lines and the iterative formula $x_{n+1} = x_n - f(x_n)/f'(x_n)$ to generate a sequence of approximate solutions to the equation $f(x) = 0$.

irrational quantities, and a remarkable type of calculus for this), which appeared in 1684 in the German mathematics journal *Acta Eruditorum* (Scholarly activities). Leibniz's concepts of derivative and integral corresponded with Newton's fluxions and fluents. His superior notations of dx, $\dfrac{dy}{dx}$, and $\int y$ made the concepts of differentials, derivatives, and integrals easier to understand and to manipulate. The members of the English mathematical community who had read Newton's unpublished manuscripts accused Leibniz of stealing Newton's ideas and presenting them as his own. The passionate dispute between English and continental European mathematicians over the priority for the invention of calculus lasted into the late 18th century. Mathematicians today recognize Newton and Leibniz as independent coinventors of the theory of calculus.

Additional Mathematical Treatises

In 1667, Newton wrote a geometrical treatise titled *Enumeratio linearum tertii ordinis* (Classification of curves of the third degree) that remained unpublished until 1704, when he included it as an appendix to his major work on optics. In this treatise, he presented a classification of cubic curves into 72 classes, genders, and orders. He also described how to generate all the conic sections as projections of a circle onto an infinite plane. The final section of the treatise explained how to use cubic equations to analyze plane curves of higher degree with particular attention to their asymptotes, nodes, and cusps.

During the 10-year period from 1673 to 1683, the weekly lectures that Newton gave as Lucasian professor of mathematics focused on algebra and number theory. These lectures were printed in 1707 under the title *Arithmetica universalis* (Universal arithmetic). In the course of several of these presentations, he generalized Descartes's technique for determining the positive real solutions to a polynomial equation with integer coefficients. His more general method determined all rational solutions and investigated the imaginary roots of such polynomials.

Newton introduced further refinements to his theory of calculus in his 1691 treatise, *Tractus de quadratura curvarum* (Treatise on the quadrature of curves), which he published as a second appendix to his 1704 work on optics. He presented a more convenient notation in which $\dot{y}$ and $\ddot{y}$ represented the first and second fluxions of the function y. As replacements for his earlier infinitesimal increments, he introduced the concept of ultimate ratios of evanescent quantities, marking the first use of the sophisticated notion of limits in the theory of calculus. In his analysis of infinite series, he addressed issues of convergence, another idea whose development was essential to the maturation of calculus. This treatise also introduced infinite series in which the coefficient of the nth term was determined by the nth fluxion, a concept further developed by English mathematician Brook Taylor and now known as Taylor series.

In 1696, Newton responded to an international challenge posed by Swiss mathematician Johann Bernoulli. The contest asked for the solution of the brachistochrone problem—to find the shortest path between two nonvertical points under the force of gravity. Newton solved the problem in a day, giving the solution as the cycloid curve—the path traced by a point on a circle as the circle rolls along a straight line. In the May 1697 edition of the journal *Acta Eruditorum*, Bernoulli published Newton's solution along with his own and those of Leibniz and Bernoulli's brother Jacob. After this contest, Newton's mathematical activities consisted of revising his earlier works or defending his priority for the discovery of calculus.

A New Theory of Light

During his final year at Trinity College, Newton began conducting optical experiments and formulating a new theory of light. The prevailing scientific theory, first pronounced in the third century B.C.E. by the Greek philosopher Aristotle, asserted that white light was a simple homogeneous entity that was fundamentally different than colored light. The chromatic aberrations around the edges of images generated by refracting telescope lenses convinced Newton that the theory was flawed. In his dormitory room, he conducted experiments passing rays of light through prisms to separate the

By passing a beam of sunlight through prisms, Newton proved that white light includes different types of rays that refract at different angles to produce the spectrum of colors. *(The Granger Collection)*

beam into a spectrum of colors. This and similar experiments that he conducted during the next several years led him to the conclusion that white light was a heterogeneous mixture of different types of rays that refracted at different angles to produce the spectrum of colors.

In January 1670, Newton presented his theory of light in his first course of lectures as Lucasian professor. He built and demonstrated a reflecting telescope that magnified images 40 times without chromatic distortion. In recognition of his theory of light and his reflecting telescope, England's national academy of scientists, the Royal Society of London for the Improvement of Natural Knowledge, elected him a member in January 1672. The following month, they printed his first published scientific article, "New theory about light and color," in their journal, *Philosophical Transactions of the Royal Society*. In this paper, Newton described the experiments he had conducted with prisms during the previous eight years and proposed a corpuscular theory of light asserting that light consisted of the motion of small particles. This controversial claim led to a protracted public dispute with English physicist Robert Hooke, who had theorized that light traveled in waves. Although his particle theory became widely accepted for two centuries, the public controversy with Hooke and other scientists contributed to Newton's nervous breakdown in 1678 and led to his refusal to publish any further scientific discoveries throughout most of his professional career.

In 1704, a year after Hooke's death, Newton published a full account of his optical researches in the work *Optiks: or, a treatise of the reflexions, refractions, inflexions and colours of light. Also two treatises of the species and magnitude of curvilinear figures.* Proceeding from the definitions of basic terms such as *ray of light, refraction, reflection,* and *angle of incidence* and the statements of fundamental axioms about the geometric properties of reflection and refraction, Newton described the extensive set of experiments he conducted and the conclusions he drew from their results. His experiments included separating white light into colored beams using prisms, bending light with the use of lenses, and passing light rays through multiple mediums of different densities, thicknesses, and colors. He described the mechanics of human vision, the phenomenon of rainbows, and the distortion of images produced by refracting telescopes. The concentric rings that he observed in experiments with two transparent surfaces almost touching each other are now called Newton's rings. To explain his observations, he used both wave and particle theories of light. Although not all his conclusions were correct, his modern theory of light, his reflecting telescope, and his scientific method of reasoning from mathematical principles and experimental results represented significant contributions to the advancement of science.

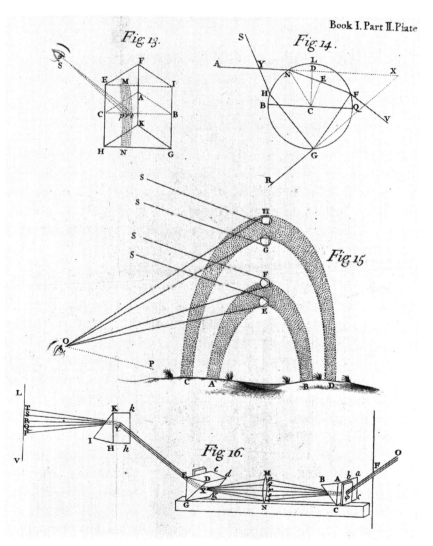

In his 1704 treatise, *Optiks,* Newton explained a range of visual phenomena, including the rainbow, the double Icelandic spar, and prism refraction. *(Library of Congress)*

Laws of Motion and the Principle of Universal Gravitation

While developing his theories of fluxions and optics in the period from 1664 to 1666, Newton also investigated the scientific principles that explained motion and gravity. Revising and extending the theories proposed by Italian scientist Galileo Galilei, Newton stated three laws of motion:

1. An object at rest tends to stay at rest while an object in motion tends to continue its motion in a straight line.
2. Force equals mass times acceleration.
3. To every action, there is an equal and opposite reaction.

Devising and interpreting the results of many experiments with moving objects, he accurately explained a wide range of phenomena as mathematical consequences of these basic principles. His analysis so generalized and clarified Galileo's ideas on motion that Newton's three laws of motion became the fundamental principles of the theory of kinematics.

Newton traced the origins of his theory of gravity to an incident that occurred while he was at home during the plague years. He told the now-famous story that the inspiration for his theory of gravity came to him when an apple fell from a tree and hit him on the head. Observing that the apple fell toward the center of the Earth, he theorized that the Earth exerted an invisible force that attracted all objects toward its center. He further hypothesized that the Earth's gravity was the force responsible for keeping the Moon in its orbit. Italian scientist Nicolaus Copernicus had theorized that moons and planets traveled in elliptic orbits, and German scientist Johannes Kepler had derived three mathematical principles to describe their motion on these elliptic paths. Combining their ideas with his concept of gravitational attraction, Newton reasoned that the force of the Earth's gravity on the Moon was inversely proportional to the distance between the two bodies. His calculations supported this theory.

In 1684, English astronomer Edmond Halley informed Newton that he, Hooke, and Sir Christopher Wren had each proposed that the elliptic orbits of the planets were due to the inverse-square attractions between the planets and the Sun. Newton told Halley that he had also made this same discovery and had mathematically proved it. During the next several months, he wrote out his explanations and in November 1684 sent Halley a 10-page manuscript titled *De motu corporum in gyram* (On the motion of bodies in an orbit). In this brief document, he explained how the inverse-square law of attraction forced the planets to orbit in elliptical paths, and he derived Kepler's three laws of planetary motion as consequences of this principle.

Through Halley's encouragement, Newton expanded his thoughts into a larger treatise entitled *Philosophiae naturalis principia mathematica* (*Mathematical Principles of Natural Philosophy*), which the Royal Society published in 1687. This three-volume work provided a full treatment of his new physics and its applications to astronomy. The first book, titled *De motu corporum in gyrum* (On the motion of bodies in an orbit), presented a mathematical treatment of the three laws of motion. He stated the law of universal gravitation that all matter attracts other matter with a force proportional to the product of their masses and inversely proportional to the square of the distance between them, a law that is written algebraically as

$F = G \ \dfrac{m_1 m_2}{d^2}$. Applying this principle to a variety of situations, he

proved that the force of gravity causes objects to travel in parabolic paths near the surface of the Earth and in elliptic or hyperbolic paths further away. He also proved that a uniformly dense spherical body exerts the same gravitational force of attraction as a single point having the same mass located at the center of the sphere. By establishing the mathematical basis of these fundamental principles, he provided a firm foundation for the other conclusions of his theory of motion. Book II, titled *De motu corporum liber secundus* (Second book on the motion of bodies), extended these ideas to the motion of pendulums, the density and compression of gases and liquid, and the motion of waves in fluids. These results enabled him to point out major flaws in Descartes's vortex theory of the universe. The third book, titled *De systemate mundi* (On the system of the world), applied the universal theory of gravity to the solar system.

By observing the motions of the planets, he calculated their masses, their relative densities, and any irregularities in their shape. He also explained the paths of comets and how the locations of the Sun and the Moon affected the heights of high and low tides.

Principia was a masterpiece that established Newton as an international scientific leader and set the direction for scientific investigation for the next century. As the influential work became known, scientists embraced its rigorously demonstrated theories and its methods of experimental observation combined with mathematical reasoning. Although only 300 copies of the first edition were printed, by 1789 *Principia* had been reissued in 18 editions and had appeared in more than 70 popular versions in six different languages. A century after Newton wrote *Principia*, French mathematician Joseph-Louis Lagrange called the work the greatest achievement of the human mind, while his countryman Pierre-Simon de Laplace judged that the treatise deserved a preeminent place above all other products of human genius.

Activities beyond Mathematics and Physics

In addition to his work in mathematics and physics, Newton pursued interests in alchemy and theology. Attempting to discover a method for converting common chemicals into gold, he built furnaces and experimented with various combinations of substances. His unpublished writings on these alchemy experiments totaled more than a million words. He produced a similarly large collection of manuscripts on his analysis of biblical passages, including a reconstruction of the floor plan of the temple in Jerusalem. His works in theology included *Observations upon the prophecies of Daniel, and the Apocalypse of St. John*, a treatise that was not published until 1733.

After experiencing a second nervous breakdown in 1693, Newton significantly reduced his research activities and became involved in nonacademic endeavors. He had experienced a taste of politics in 1689, when he served as a Member of the Convention Parliament that declared William and Mary the legal successors to the throne of James II. In 1696, he accepted the position of Warden of the Royal Mint, where he reorganized and improved the mint's operation. When he was promoted to Master of the Mint in 1699, he introduced a new set of coins whose deeper reliefs and milled edges effectively combated the practices of clipping and counterfeiting. Since he earned a commission on the amount of money that the mint coined, he became a wealthy man, drawing an average annual income of £2,000. In 1701, he resigned his fellowship at Trinity College and his professorship at Cambridge University. The Royal Society elected him to his first of 24 terms as their president in 1703. Queen Anne knighted him Sir Isaac Newton in 1705 in recognition of his scientific achievements, making him the first scientist to receive this honor. He died in London on March 20, 1727, at the age of 84 and was buried as a national hero in Westminster Abbey.

Conclusion

When Newton was asked how he was able to achieve his significant advances in mathematics and science, he replied that if he had seen further than others it was because he had stood on the shoulders of giants. In his development of the general theory of calculus, the laws of motion, and the universal principle of gravitation, he synthesized the discoveries of his predecessors and contemporaries, combining them with his own ideas to formulate more general theories. His insistence that scientific theories were not valid unless they were supported by experimental evidence and mathematics proof gained widespread acceptance throughout the European scientific community and became the new standard for scientific investigation. The calculus he invented remains the primary technique for analyzing continuous functions and still forms the central core of the mathematical education of college and university students. Because his many original and significant discoveries demonstrated such powerful insight, mathematicians rank Newton with Archimedes of Syracuse and Carl Friedrich Gauss as one of the three greatest mathematicians of all time.

FURTHER READING

Bell, Eric T. "On the Seashore." In *Men of Mathematics*, 90–116. New York: Simon and Schuster, 1965. Chapter 6 presents an informative biography and evaluation of his mathematical work.

Boyer, Carl B. "Newton and Leibniz." In *A History of Mathematics*, 2nd ed., 391–414. New York: Wiley, 1991. Chapter 19 presents biographies of the two mathematicians and their roles in the development of calculus.

Dunham, William. "A Gem from Isaac Newton." In *Journey through Genius: The Great Theorems of Mathematics*, 155–183. New York: Wiley, 1990. Chapter 7 discusses Newton's proof of the binomial theorem and the accompanying historical context.

———. "Knighted Newton." In *The Mathematical Universe: An Alphabetical Journey through the Great Proof, Problems, and Personalities*, 129–142. New York: Wiley, 1994. Chapter K discusses Newton's invention of calculus in an historical context and highlights Newton's method for iteratively approximating the solutions to equations.

Moore, Patrick. "Isaac Newton, 1643–1727: English Mathematician and Physicist." In *Notable Mathematicians: From Ancient Times to the Present*, edited by Robyn V. Young, 367–369. Detroit, Mich.: Gale, 1998. Short but informative profile of Newton and his work.

O'Connor, J. J., and E. F. Robertson. "Sir Isaac Newton," MacTutor History of Mathematics Archive," University of Saint Andrews. Available online. URL: http://www-groups.dcs.st-andrews.ac.uk/~history/Mathematicians/Newton.html. Accessed January 27, 2003. Online biography, from the University of Saint Andrews, Scotland.

Rattansi, P. M. *Isaac Newton and Gravity*. East Sussex, U.K.: Priory Press, 1974. An informative rendition of his life with a simplified but accurate description of his scientific discoveries; for younger audiences.

Reimer, Luetta, and Wilbert Reimer. "The Short Giant: Isaac Newton." In *Mathematicians Are People, Too: Stories from the Lives of Great Mathematicians*, 62–71. Parsippany, N.J.: Seymour, 1990. Life story with historical facts and fictionalized dialogue; intended for elementary school students.

Youschkevitch, A. P. "Newton, Isaac." In *Dictionary of Scientific Biography*, vol. 10, edited by Charles C. Gillispie, 42–103. New York: Scribner, 1972. Encyclopedic biography including a detailed description of his writings on mathematics and physics.

7

Gottfried Leibniz

(1646–1716)

Gottfried Leibniz published the first research papers on the general theory of calculus and invented a calculating machine. (*Joh.Gottfr. Auerbach as viv. Delin Viennae 1714. Joh. Elias Haid sc. 1781. Aug. Vind., AIP Emilio Segrè Visual Archives*)

Coinventor of Calculus

Gottfried Leibniz (pronounced LĪP-nitz), a voracious reader and prolific correspondent, engaged the leading European scholars on matters of mathematics, philosophy, physics, and theology. Synthesizing the techniques of other mathematicians with his original ideas, he invented a general theory of differential and integral calculus. He proposed a system of formal logic, introduced the concept of determinants, and summed infinite series. In nonmathematical disciplines, he expounded the theory that the universe was composed of fundamental units that he called monads, provided explanations for the phenomenon of motion, and argued for the existence of a benevolent God.

Family and Education

Gottfried Wilhelm Leibniz was born on July 1, 1646, in Leipzig, Germany, to Friedrich Leibniz, a professor of moral philosophy at the University of Leipzig, and Catherina Schmuck, his third wife. His father died when he was six years old, leaving his mother to raise Leibniz, his half-brother, Johann Friedrich, his half-sister, Anna Rosina, and his sister, Anna Catherina.

From 1653 to 1661, Leibniz attended the Nicolai School in Leipzig, where he learned history, literature, Latin, Greek, theology, and logic. With unrestricted access to his father's library, he read extensively on many subjects, a practice that he continued throughout his life. He taught himself Latin before he encountered the subject at school, enabling him to read philosophical and religious works from an array of Catholic and Protestant writers. By the time he graduated, he was composing poems in Latin and formulating his own philosophical ideas.

Leibniz earned four college degrees during the next five years. In 1661, he enrolled in a two-year program of classical studies at the University of Leipzig, taking courses in Latin, Hebrew, Greek, and rhetoric. He earned his bachelor's degree in 1663 by writing a thesis titled *De principio individui* (On the principle of the individual), a preliminary treatment of the philosophical theory of monads that he more fully developed over the next 50 years. During the summer of 1663, he visited the University of Jena in Austria, where he took courses in geometry and algebra. This first experience with higher-level mathematics impressed on him the importance of mathematical proof. Returning to Leipzig, he earned a master's degree in philosophy in 1664 and a bachelor's degree in law the following year.

In preparation for his doctoral degree in law and a possible career as a law professor, he prepared two dissertations. For his *habitationsschrift*, the thesis required to lecture at a German university, he wrote "Dissertatio de arte combinatorial" (Dissertation on the combinatorial art), in which he attempted to reduce all reasoning and discovery to a combination of basic elements such as numbers, letters, sounds, and colors. He eventually developed this idea into a system of formal mathematical logic. For his doctoral thesis, he composed "Disputatio de casibus perplexis" (Disputation on perplexing cases), in which he discussed intricacies of the law. When the University of Leipzig refused to grant him his doctoral degree on the grounds that he was too young, he transferred to the University of Altdorf in Nuremburg, where he was granted his terminal degree in November 1666.

Service to Royal Patrons

Soon after earning his doctoral degree, Leibniz embarked on a lifelong career of service to a sequence of royal patrons, enabling him to travel, study, write, and mingle with international scholars. Rejecting the offer of a law professorship at the University of Altdorf, he temporarily accepted a position as secretary to the Rosicrucian Society of Nuremburg, a group of alchemists searching for a method to convert common chemicals into gold. From 1667 to 1673, he entered into the service of the first of his five royal patrons, Elector Johann Philipp von Schönborn, the prince of Mainz. As a legal adviser and an assessor in the Court of Appeals, he wrote position papers for the elector, resolved general legal problems, and developed the elector's program for reform of the civil laws of the Holy Roman Empire, the loose confederation of central European states. His responsibilities enabled him to correspond with scholars throughout Europe and establish contacts with the secretaries of the leading academic societies. During his lifetime, he wrote 15,000 letters to more than 600 colleagues, discussing topics from a wide range of academic disciplines.

Two diplomatic missions to Paris and London enabled him to meet international scholars and participate in intellectual discussions. In 1672, the elector sent him to Paris in an unsuccessful attempt to persuade Louis XIV, king of France, to conquer Egypt, establish a colony in North Africa, and build a canal across the isthmus of Suez. While in Paris, he developed friendships with mathematicians Christiaan Huygens and Pierre de Carcavi, who introduced him to other members of the Académie Royale des Sciences (Royal Academy of Sciences) and provided him access to unpublished papers written by mathematicians Blaise Pascal and René Descartes. In 1673, he traveled to London on another diplomatic mission to encourage peace negotiations between England and the Netherlands. During this trip, he met mathematician John Pell, established contacts with other scientists and philosophers, and was elected to the Royal Society of London.

When elector Johann Philipp died in 1673, Leibniz established a private law practice in Paris but spent most of his time studying mathematics. From 1676 to 1679, he held a sequence of positions in Hanover, Germany, in the service of Johann Friedrich, duke of Brunswick-Lüneburg, as a member of the duke's personal staff, legal adviser, librarian, consultant on engineering projects, court councillor, judge, and superintendent of the mint. At the duke's request, he designed windmill-powered pumps using pipes filled with compressed air to drain water from the Harz silver mine. Although the project ended in failure, the observations he compiled led him to form the geological hypothesis that the Earth had at one time been a mass of molten rock.

From 1680 to 1698, Leibniz worked for Ernst August, who had succeeded his brother as duke of Brunswick after Johann Friedrich's death in 1679. The new duke commissioned him to write a genealogy of the house of Brunswick to support the family's regal claim. The research for this project took him on a three-year tour of Europe to Munich, Vienna, Rome, Florence, Venice, Bologna, and Modena. In Vienna, he discussed plans for economic and scientific reforms with Leopold I, the Holy Roman Emperor. During his visit to Rome, he turned down an offer to become librarian at the Vatican and was elected to membership in the Accademia fisicomatematica (Academy of Mathematical Physics), the Italian mathematical society. By 1690, he had compiled nine volumes of archival material that successfully established an ancestral link between the house of Este and the Guelph family, of which the house of Brunswick was a part. This research resulted in the 1692 elevation of the duke to the status of elector, one of the German princes who are entitled to vote in elections for the new emperor of the Holy Roman Empire.

Georg Ludwig, who succeeded Ernst August as elector of Brunswick in 1698, employed Liebniz for the last 18 years of his life writing the family history of the house of Brunswick. With his intellectual talents underutilized on this project, Leibniz found an additional patron in Sophia Charlotte, electress of Bradenburg and daughter of Ernst August. She hired Leibniz as a private tutor and privy councillor and also assigned him the task of establishing a scholarly academy in Berlin. In 1700, he created and became president of the Bradenburg Society of Science that 10 years later became l'Académie Royale des Sciences et des Belles-Lettres de Berlin (Royal Academy of Sciences and Beautiful Letters in Berlin). Beginning in 1712, he worked to establish similar academies in St. Petersburg, Russia, and Vienna, Austria. Although Georg Ludwig became George I, king of England, in 1714, he did not offer Leibniz a position in his English court, requesting instead that he remain in Hanover finishing the family history that he never completed.

Leibniz's varied responsibilities for his series of patrons enabled him to correspond with a wide network of intellectuals, establish working relationships with learned colleagues in many countries, remain abreast of the activities of scholarly academies, and access the latest research of international scholars. These opportunities, combined with his voracious appetite for reading and his willingness to engage in intensive periods of research, enabled him to develop significant theories and methods in many academic disciplines.

General Theory of Calculus

During the 1670s and 1680s, Leibniz produced his greatest mathematical achievement—the development of a general theory of calculus. While visiting Paris in 1672, he read papers on infinite series by Flemish mathematician Gregory of Saint-Vincent and Pascal's treatise on methods for finding areas of segments of a circle. In 1673, Pell shared with him other recent results on infinite series, and Huygens helped him to learn advanced methods of higher geometry. With this mathematical background, he developed a general method of tangents to find areas under curves. Pascal, Pierre de Fermat, Gilles de Roberval, Isaac Barrow, Bonaventura Cavalieri, Evangelista Torricelli, and other European mathematicians

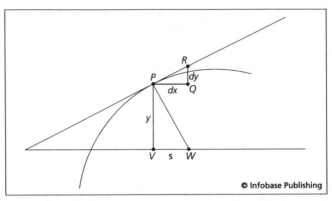

© Infobase Publishing

The method of subtangents that formed the core of Leibniz's theory of calculus was based on the relationship between the characteristic triangle *PQR* and the length of the subtangent segment *VW* as expressed in the equation $\int \sigma dx = \int y\, dy$.

had devised limited methods for finding areas under specific classes of curves. Leibniz's general method of tangents constituted a system of integration (sometimes called quadrature) that successfully applied to all the cases treatable by the entire collection of known techniques.

In a 1674 letter to Huygens, Leibniz announced that by using the infinite series for the arctangent function, he had extended his methods of integration to apply to areas inside a segment of a circle, areas inside a segment of a hyperbola, and areas related to the cycloid curve. Within a year, he developed the basic features of calculus, constructing a derivative operator to find the slope of the tangent line at any point on a curve and further generalizing his method of integration to an infinite sum of rectangles that produced the area under a curve. He developed the notations dx, $\dfrac{dy}{dx}$, and $\int y$ for the concepts of differential, derivative, and integral. After several failed attempts, he correctly derived the product rule for derivatives: $d(uv) = u \cdot dv + v \cdot du$. His major breakthrough during this year was the discovery of the inverse relationship between the operations of differentiation and integration, the principle known as the fundamental theorem of calculus. This key idea that was missing in all the papers he had read on techniques for determining tangents and areas formed the overarching theme that unified the collection of diverse techniques into a general theory of calculus. By the fall of 1676, Leibniz had proven the power rule for derivatives $d(x^n) = nx^{n-1} \, dx$ for both integer and fractional values of n and the chain rule that applied to sequential operations. He composed a manuscript that explained all his ideas on calculus and circulated it to several colleagues but never published the work.

Through an exchange of four letters with English mathematician Sir Isaac Newton in 1676 and 1677, Leibniz inquired about some of the details of Newton's method of infinite series and shared some of his results about integration. Neither he nor Newton was aware that they had both independently developed equivalent theories of calculus. Between 1664 and 1666, Newton had developed a method of fluxions and fluents that corresponded to Leibniz's method of derivatives and integrals. Because Newton had not yet published any description of his method of fluxions, Leibniz continued to develop and perfect his methods under the belief that his research was original and innovative.

A set of three papers published in the German mathematics journal *Acta Eruditorum* (Scholarly activities) during the 1680s comprised the formal announcement of Leibniz's general theory of calculus. The 1682 paper "De vera proportione circuli ad quadratum circumscriptum in numeris rationalibus" (On some circular proportions to quadratic circumscription in rational numbers) provided a concise summary of the main results of his method for the quadrature of the circle but did not fully reveal his system of calculus. Two years later, he published "Nova methodus pro maximis et minimis, itemque tangentibus, quae nec fractus nec irrationales quantitates moratur, et singulare pro illis calculi genus" (A new method for maxima and minima, as well as tangents, which is obstructed neither by fractional nor irrational quantities, and a remarkable type of calculus for this). In this landmark paper, he gave a full description of his method of derivatives, publicly introducing the terms *derivative*, *differential*, *differentiation*, and *calculus* as well as the $d\,(\ )$ and $\dfrac{dy}{dx}$ notations for the differential and the derivative. He presented the power rule, product rule, and quotient rule for derivatives without any proofs and explained his method for determining algebraic integrals of algebraic functions. Geometrically motivating the idea of derivative as the slope of a line tangent to a curve, he showed how to use the derivative to find the extreme points on a curve and how to use the second derivative to classify them as maximums or minimums. The companion paper, "De geometria recondita et analysi indivisibilium atque infinitorum" (On the secrets of geometry and analysis of indivisible and infinite quantities), appearing in 1686, explained the process of integral calculus and the fundamental theorem of calculus. The paper presented the first published use of the elongated "S" symbol $\int$ and the notation $\int y dx$ for the integral.

In the next 10 years, Leibniz developed several additional calculus techniques. By 1691, he had obtained infinite series to represent the trigonometric functions $\sin(x)$ and $\cos(x)$, the natural logarithmic function $\ln(1 + x)$, and its exponential inverse function. In 1693, he communicated his method for solving differential equations using the method of undetermined coefficients. Two years later, he explained his technique for differentiating exponential functions of the form y^x. In 1702, he circulated methods for finding integrals of

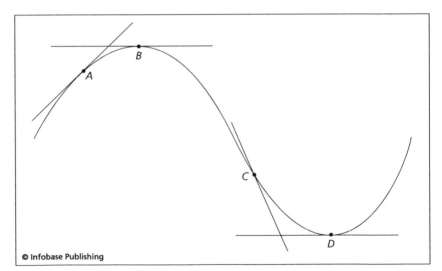

© Infobase Publishing

In his major treatise on differential calculus, Leibniz explained that the derivative measured the slope of the tangent line. When the slope was positive or negative, the graph was rising (A) or falling (C); when the slope was zero, the graph could take its maximum (B) or minimum (D) values.

rational functions, and in 1704, he expanded them to special cases of irrational functions.

The remainder of his letters and papers on the subject of calculus dealt with the controversial debate between mathematicians in England and in continental Europe concerning the priority for the invention of calculus. English mathematicians accused Leibniz of stealing Newton's ideas, while continental mathematicians pointed to Leibniz's different notation, terminology, and earlier publication to substantiate his claim of originality. In 1702, Leibniz wrote "A justification of the calculus of the infinitely small" in an attempt to fully explain his methods and to clarify the sequence of events that led him to his discoveries. The debate persisted into the late 18th century. Mathematicians today recognize Newton and Leibniz as independent coinventors of the theory of calculus.

Additional Mathematical Discoveries

In addition to the development of calculus, Leibniz made other contributions to mathematics. In the early 1670s, he designed a

Leibniz designed a calculating machine capable of adding, subtracting, multiplying, dividing, and taking square roots. *(The Image Works)*

mechanical calculator capable of adding, subtracting, multiplying, dividing, and taking square roots through the interactions of a series of gears and springs. He built an incomplete model in 1672 that he demonstrated at a meeting of the Royal Society of London in 1673. Realizing that his design was more advanced than the available technology, he soon turned his attention to other projects. The first practical calculating machine, constructed in 1774 by P. M. Hahn, was substantially based on Leibniz's design.

While investigating the arithmetic of complex numbers in 1774, Leibniz presented the equation $\sqrt{1+\sqrt{-3}} + \sqrt{1-\sqrt{-3}} = \sqrt{6}$. By squaring both sides of the equation and following the standard rules of arithmetic in a strictly formal manner, he demonstrated the validity of the equation. Generalizing this result, he reasoned that the sum of any pair of conjugate complex expressions such as $\sqrt{a+\sqrt{-b}}$ and $\sqrt{a-\sqrt{-b}}$ will always produce a real number.

Leibniz's early work on calculus was closely related to investigations of infinite series. In 1775, he produced a creative solution for the infinite sum of the reciprocals of the triangular numbers:

$$S = \frac{1}{1} + \frac{1}{3} + \frac{1}{6} + \frac{1}{10} + \frac{1}{15} + \ldots + \frac{1}{n(n+1)/2} + \ldots .$$ Dividing both

sides of the equation by 2, he realized that each resulting fraction could be expressed as the difference of two simpler fractions as

$$\frac{S}{2} = \frac{1}{2} + \frac{1}{6} + \frac{1}{12} + \frac{1}{20} + \frac{1}{30} + \ldots + \frac{1}{n(n+1)} + \ldots$$

$$= \left(1 - \frac{1}{2}\right) + \left(\frac{1}{2} - \frac{1}{3}\right) + \left(\frac{1}{3} - \frac{1}{4}\right) + \left(\frac{1}{4} - \frac{1}{5}\right) + \left(\frac{1}{5} - \frac{1}{6}\right) + \cdots \left(\frac{1}{n} - \frac{1}{n+1}\right) + \cdots .$$

Regrouping the terms so that adjacent fractions canceled out, he showed that $\frac{S}{2}$ = 1, or that the sum totaled to 2. The following year, by integrating the area under one quarter of a circle, Leibniz produced the summation $\frac{\pi}{4} = 1 - \frac{1}{3} + \frac{1}{5} - \frac{1}{7} + \frac{1}{9} - \frac{1}{11} + \ldots,$ which expressed the value of the transcendental constant π in terms of a combination of all the odd integers.

For situations involving systems of linear equations, Leibniz introduced new notation that that he used to determine whether the system had any solutions. With the equations written in a standard form such as

$$10 + 2x + 3y = 0$$
$$13 + 7x + 5y = 0$$
$$15 + x + 4y = 0,$$

he used the notation 2_0 to refer to the zeroth coefficient in the second equation (13) and 3_2 to indicate the coefficient of the second variable in the third equation (4). Using these notations, he established an equation that the coefficients had to satisfy in order for the system of equation to have a solution. That equation,

$$1_0 \cdot 2_1 \cdot 3_2 + 1_1 \cdot 2_2 \cdot 3_0 + 1_2 \cdot 2_0 \cdot 3_1 = 1_0 \cdot 2_2 \cdot 3_1 + 1_1 \cdot 2_0 \cdot 3_2 + 1_2 \cdot 2_1 \cdot 3_0,$$

is equivalent to the requirement that the modern concept of the determinant be equal to zero. His innovative work on determinants, completed in 1684, remained unpublished until 1850.

Leibniz experimented with a binary system of arithmetic in which he used only the symbols 0 and 1 to express numbers as sums of powers of 2. In this base-2 notation, 1101 represented $1 \cdot 2^3 + 1 \cdot 2^2 + 0 \cdot 2^1 + 1 \cdot 2^0 = 8 + 4 + 0 + 1 = 13$, and 10.11 indicated the fractional value $1 \cdot 2^1 + 0 \cdot 2^0 + 1 \cdot 2^{-1} + 1 \cdot 2^{-2} = 2 + 0 + \dfrac{1}{2} + \dfrac{1}{4} = 2\dfrac{3}{4}$. Leibniz gave a theological interpretation to his binary system of arithmetic, envisioning 1 as representing God, who created all things from nothing by endowing them with portions of his spirit. He described his ideas on binary notation in the 1701 treatise *Essay d'une nouvelle science des nombres* (Essay on a new science of numbers) that he submitted to the Académie Royale des Sciences on the occasion of his election to membership in that body. Mathematicians in the 20th century more fully developed the methods of binary arithmetic to provide the means for representing all information in modern electronic computers.

Other than calculus, Leibniz's most significant mathematical contribution was in the area of logic, where he attempted to develop an algebra of thought that reduced all logical argumentation to a symbolic form. In his 1666 thesis, *Dissertatio de arte combinatoria* (Dissertation on the combinational art), he had introduced the idea of a universal characteristic that would lead to such a system of formal logic. He worked to develop universal symbols to represent a small number of fundamental concepts and to create logical operations that expressed all human thoughts as combinations of these universal symbols. With such a system, truth and error would be matters of correct and erroneous computations, while routine calculations would lead to new discoveries. His partial success included the development of the concepts of identity, the null class, logical multiplication, negation, and class inclusion that he developed in 1679 but did not publish until 1701. In the 19th century, English mathematician George Boole seized on Leibniz's idea, creating a boolean algebra in which logical operations such as "and," "or," "not," and "implication" are used to build compound statements from simpler ones.

Philosophy, Dynamics, and Theology

Leibniz was an intellectual with a broad range of interests beyond the boundaries of mathematics. He published a number of theories in philosophy, dynamics, and theology that engaged the leading scholars of those disciplines. In his 1714 treatise, *Monadologia* (System of monads), he proposed the theory that the all objects are composed of innumerable tiny units called monads whose interaction explained all aspects of the physical and spiritual world. He wrote position papers in theology and helped to organize two conferences in Hanover during the 1680s in an attempt to reunite the Catholic and Protestant churches. In his 1710 treatise, *Essais de théodicée sur la bonté de Dieu, la liberté de l'homme et l'origine du mal* (Theological essays on the goodness of God, the freedom of man, and the origin of evil), he argued for the existence of a benevolent God, addressed the existence of evil in an imperfect world, and discussed the idea of optimism arguing that reason and faith were not incompatible. In his 1619 two-part treatise on dynamics titled *Essay de dynamique* (Essay on dynamics) and *Specimen dynamicum* (Dynamical specimen), he explained kinetic energy, potential energy, and momentum in scientific terms supported by his theory of calculus.

After a long life as an active participant in the international community of intellectuals, Leibniz died in relative obscurity, suffering from arthritis, gout, and colic, on November 14, 1716. None of the academies that he helped to establish or of which he was a member published an official obituary. No representative from the royal courts to which he gave a lifetime of service attended his funeral on December 14.

Conclusion

The innovative mathematical ideas that Leibniz initiated have had profound effects on the progress of mathematics, science, and technology. The calculus that Leibniz and Newton invented remains the primary technique for analyzing continuous functions in all scientific disciplines and still forms the central core of the mathematical education of college and university students. The mathematical system of logic that he started to create and the binary system of computation that he promoted form the logical basis for the storage and manipulation of data in all modern computers. His concept of a determinant plays a crucial role in linear algebra and the solutions of systems of equations.

FURTHER READING

Bell, Eric T. "Master of All Trades." In *Men of Mathematics*, 117–130. New York: Simon and Schuster, 1965. Chapter 7 presents a biography and evaluation of Leibniz's mathematical work.

Boyer, Carl B. "Newton and Leibniz." In *A History of Mathematics*, 2nd ed., 391–414. New York: Wiley, 1991. Chapter 19 presents biographies of the two mathematicians and their roles in the development of calculus.

Carpenter, Jill. "Gottfried Wilhelm von Leibniz, 1646–1716: German Logician and Philosopher." In *Notable Mathematicians: From Ancient Times to the Present*, edited by Robyn V. Young, 310–312. Detroit, Mich.: Gale, 1998. Informative profile of Leibniz and his work.

Dunham, William. "Lost Leibniz." In *The Mathematical Universe: An Alphabetical Journey through the Great Proof, Problems, and*

Personalities, 143–158. New York: Wiley, 1994. Chapter L discusses Leibniz's method of integration and the accompanying historical context.

Hoffman, Joseph. "Leibniz Gottfried Wilhelm." In *Dictionary of Scientific Biography*, vol. 8, edited by Charles C. Gillispie, 149–168. New York: Scribner, 1972. Encyclopedic biography including a detailed description of his writings on mathematics and other disciplines.

O'Connor, J. J., and E. F. Robertson. "Gottfried Wilhelm von Leibniz," MacTutor History of Mathematics Archive, University of Saint Andrews. Available online. URL: http://www-groups. dcs.st-andrews.ac.uk/~history/Mathematicians/Leibniz.html. Accessed January 27, 2003. Online biography, from the University of Saint Andrews, Scotland.

8

Leonhard Euler

(1707–1783)

Although he was blind for much of his professional career, Leonhard Euler wrote 900 books and papers on a range of mathematical and scientific topics. *(Library of Congress)*

Leading Mathematician of the 18th Century

Although he was blind for much of his life, Leonhard Euler (pronounced LEN-erd OI-ler) was the most influential mathematician of the 18th century. As a theoretical mathematician, he made significant contributions to algebra, geometry, calculus, and number theory. As an applied mathematician and scientist, he made important discoveries in mechanics, astronomy, optics, and shipbuilding.

Euler's innovative ideas led to the development of new branches of mathematics, including graph theory, ring theory, calculus of variations, and combinatorial topology. Through his dozens of books and almost 900 research papers, his lifetime of work continues to influence mathematics today.

Student Years, 1707–1726

Leonhard Euler was born on April 15, 1707, in the city of Basel, Switzerland, to Paul Euler, a Protestant minister, and Margaret Brucker Euler, the daughter of a minister. Although his parents encouraged him to become a minister, he felt a greater attraction to a career in mathematics. When he was a year old, his family moved to the nearby town of Riehen. As a young boy, he could memorize lists of numbers, long poems, and speeches given by famous people and could complete lengthy, involved calculations in his head. Recognizing his talents, Euler's parents sent him to live with his grandmother Brucker in the city of Basel so he could attend better schools there.

In 1720, at the age of 13, Euler was admitted to the University of Basel. There he met mathematics professor Johann Bernoulli, who had been his father's friend when the two were students together at the University of Basel. Although Euler did not take any of Bernoulli's classes, the professor selected math books for him to read and suggested problems for him to try. Every Saturday afternoon, Euler visited the professor to discuss any details that he did not understand. Through these weekly meetings, Bernoulli observed and encouraged his young student's mathematical talents.

As a philosophy major at the University of Basel, Euler studied a wide range of subjects, but he always maintained a deep interest in mathematics. For his thesis, he wrote a paper comparing the philosophical writings of René Descartes and Sir Isaac Newton, two of the greatest mathematicians of the previous century. Within four years, he completed his undergraduate and graduate courses, earning a bachelor's degree in philosophy in 1722 and a master's degree in philosophy in 1724. At the age of 17, Euler enrolled in the divinity school to study to become a minister as his parents had hoped he would. He studied Hebrew, Greek, and theology but continued to meet with Bernoulli to discuss mathematics. Eventually, the professor convinced Euler's parents that their son's mathematical talents far exceeded his potential as a minister.

Pursuing full-time mathematical studies under Bernoulli's direction, Euler made his first mathematical discoveries, finding new properties of two classes of mathematical curves. He explained these ideas in his first two research papers: "Constructio linearum isochronarum in medio quocunque resistente" (Construction of isochronous curves in a resistant medium), which appeared in the journal *Acta eruditorum* (Scholarly activities) in 1726, and "Methodus inveniendi trajectorias reciprocas algebraicas" (Method for finding algebraic reciprocal trajectories), which was published in 1727 in the same journal. After two years of intensive work, Euler completed his studies in mathematics at the University of Basel.

Early Years at St. Petersburg Academy, 1727–1741

During his years at the university, Euler had become friends with Bernoulli's son Daniel, who was seven years older than Euler. In 1725, Daniel Bernoulli had moved to Russia to become the first head of the mathematics department at St. Petersburg Academy of Sciences. This institute had been established in 1723 by Empress Catherine I, wife of Peter the Great, the ruler of Russia, to advance the study of mathematics and science. Daniel Bernoulli encouraged Euler to apply for a faculty position at the academy. Through his influence, 19-year-old Euler was offered a position to teach applications of mathematics in the department of medicine and physiology.

When he arrived in St. Petersburg for the start of the 1727 school year, Euler was informed that he had been transferred to the mathematics and physics division. He moved into a room at Bernoulli's house and lived there for a few years, an arrangement that provided the two many opportunities to discuss mathematics. To supplement his modest income at the academy, Euler served for four years as a medical lieutenant in the Russian navy.

During his first year at St. Petersburg, Euler entered a competition sponsored by the Parisian Academy of Sciences in Paris, France. The competitors were asked to determine the most efficient way to arrange the masts on a sailing ship. Euler's solution earned him second prize, the first of 12 prizes that he won in these annual problem-solving contests throughout his career.

In 1730, Euler was appointed to the position of professor of physics at the academy. Three years later, when Daniel Bernoulli moved back to Switzerland to accept a position at another university, the 26-year-old Euler became head of the mathematics department. In 1734, he married Katharina Gsell, the daughter of a Swiss painter who had moved to Russia. He and Katharina would be married for 40 years and have 13 children. Euler, who enjoyed playing with and reading to his children, spent many evenings doing his mathematical research while holding a baby in one arm. Unfortunately, as was common at the time, eight of the children died at very young ages from various diseases.

In 1735, Euler made a mathematical discovery that made him famous throughout Europe. He determined a way to add the fractions $1 + \frac{1}{4} + \frac{1}{9} + \frac{1}{16} + \frac{1}{25} + \cdots$. This infinite series can be written in the abbreviated form $\sum \frac{1}{n^2}$ because it is the sum of $\frac{1}{1^2} + \frac{1}{2^2} + \frac{1}{3^2} + \frac{1}{4^2} + \frac{1}{5^2} \cdots$. This problem was known as the Basel problem because Johann Bernoulli's older brother, Jakob, who had also been a mathematics professor at the University of Basel, had publicized the problem and challenged all mathematicians to solve it. In the 90 years that mathematicians worked on this problem, they had been able to determine that, even though there were infinitely many terms, the sum did not exceed 2 and that the total seemed to be close to 1.64. Euler showed that the sum added up to exactly $\frac{\pi^2}{6}$, which is approximately 1.644934. His proof was regarded as a masterpiece of logic and mathematics because it combined results about infinite products and infinite sums with properties of the trigonometric function $\sin(x)$. While working on this problem, he also determined the exact answers for the similar infinite sums with exponents of 4, 6, 8, 10, and 12 in the denominators.

After solving the Basel problem, Euler made many more mathematical discoveries, wrote papers about them, and submitted them to the mathematics journal published by St. Petersburg Academy. He wrote so many papers that in some issues of the journal half of the articles were his. Eventually, he became the editor of the journal. Since St. Petersburg Academy was run by the government, one of Euler's responsibilities as a professor there was to be a consultant to various branches of the government and military. In addition to editing, researching, and teaching, he helped to prepare maps, gave advice to the Russian navy, and tested designs for fire engines.

One of Euler's mathematical colleagues at the academy, Christian Goldbach, interested Euler in his research on number theory, the study of the properties of whole numbers. Although Goldbach left St. Petersburg after only a few years to teach at Moscow University, he and Euler kept in close contact and continued their research collaboration for their entire lives by writing frequent letters to each other.

In 1732, Euler obtained one of his first results in number theory by disproving a claim that had been made by the mathematician Pierre de Fermat about a hundred years earlier. Fermat was the most famous mathematician in the field of number theory, and, although he never published his proofs, his mathematical claims were usually correct. Fermat had claimed that if the positive integer n was a power of 2, then the number $2^n + 1$ was prime; that is, it could not be factored as the product of two integers greater than 1. Euler showed that the number $2^{32} + 1 = 4,294,967,297$ was not prime by factoring it as $(641)(6,700,417)$. His success with this problem stimulated Euler's lifelong interest in number theory.

Euler successfully researched another claim that Fermat made, the famous conjecture known as Fermat's last theorem. For 2,000 years, mathematicians had known that the equation $a^2 + b^2 = c^2$ had infinitely many positive integer solutions, such as $a = 3$, $b = 4$, $c = 5$ and $a = 5$, $b = 12$, $c = 13$. Fermat claimed that the general equation $a^n + b^n = c^n$ had no integer solutions if n was an integer greater than 2. No one had been able to find a set of three such integers, but no one had been able to prove that it was impossible to find such a set either. Euler proved that when $n = 3$, the equation had no integer solutions. His proof astounded the mathematical world, and the mathematical ideas that he developed in the proof led to the establishment of a new branch of mathematics called ring theory. In later years, other mathematicians proved similar results for other values of n, but this theorem was not fully proven until 1994 by English mathematician Andrew Wiles.

Another important contribution Euler made to number theory was the introduction of the Euler phi (pronounced FEE) function, $\phi(n)$, that he used to represent the number of integers k from 1 to n for which k and n have no common factors other than 1. Such a pair of numbers are said to be co-prime. As an example, $\phi(6) = 2$ since 6 has common factors with 2, 3, 4, and 6 but not with 1 and 5. Likewise, $\phi(12) = 4$ since 12 has common factors with 2, 3, 4, 6, 8, 9, 10, and 12 but not with 1, 5, 7, and 11. However, $\phi(19) = 18$ because 19 does not have a common factor with any smaller numbers; it is a prime number. This simple concept has become an important idea in number theory, where prime numbers and factoring are two of the key concepts.

In 1736, Euler solved the Königsberg bridge problem, another famous problem that had puzzled mathematicians for many years. The German city of Königsberg was built on four landmasses connected by seven bridges. People wondered if it was possible to go for a walk through town by crossing each bridge exactly once. Euler created an abstract representation of the problem using a graph in which each landmass was denoted by a point or vertex and each bridge from one landmass to another was represented by a curved line segment or edge.

Euler classified each vertex as an even vertex or an odd vertex based on the number of edges that met there. He then observed that if a vertex was odd, it had to be either the beginning or the end of the walking tour. Since the Königsberg graph had four odd vertices, it was not possible to construct such a walking tour. He also proved that in order to make a walking tour that started and ended at the same place, all the vertices had to be even vertices. Such a tour has come to be called an Eulerian circuit. The mathematical concepts Euler invented to solve this problem established a new branch of mathematics called graph theory, an active research area in mathematics today.

One of Euler's most highly regarded achievements during this period of years was his publication in 1736 and 1737 of the two-vol-

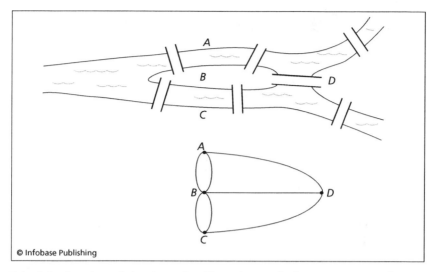

Euler introduced an abstract graph with vertices and edges to represent the seven bridges of Königsberg. In the process of solving this famous problem, he introduced the discipline of graph theory.

ume work *Mechanica* (Mechanics). In these physics books, he used calculus to explain the laws of motion and dynamics that Newton had introduced in the 17th century. He developed general methods where none had previously existed for solving problems about the motion of a mass through a vacuum and through a resisting medium. He also developed new results in differential geometry and geodesy for analyzing the motion of a mass on a surface.

In 1738, at the age of 31, Euler had a severe eye infection, and within two years, he lost the sight in his right eye. Despite his impairment, he continued to write papers about shipbuilding, acoustics, and the physics of music. In 1738 and 1740, he won the grand prize in the annual problem-solving competition sponsored by the Parisian Academy of Sciences. By 1741, he had published 55 research papers and written 30 other papers that were not published during his lifetime.

After Empress Catherine I died, many people in Russia became suspicious of foreigners like Euler. They pressured the new ruler to replace all foreign-born professors with native Russian citizens. After 14 fruitful years, Euler was forced to leave St. Petersburg Academy.

Middle Years at Berlin Academy, 1741–1766

In 1741, Euler accepted an invitation from the king of Prussia, Fredrick the Great, to become a mathematics professor at the Académie Royale des Sciences et des Belles Lettres de Berlin (Royal Academy of the Sciences and Beautiful Letters of Berlin), a new institute that he was establishing in what is now Berlin, Germany. During the 25 productive years that Euler spent at the Berlin academy, he wrote 380 books and papers on a wide range of topics in pure and applied mathematics. Additionally, he served as the director of the observatory, director of the botanical gardens, and head of the department that produced maps and calendars. He eventually became the head of the academy, serving in this capacity from 1759 to 1766.

METHODUS

INVENIENDI CURVAS

MAXIMI MINIMIVE PROPRIETATE
GAUDENTES.

CAPUT PRIMUM.

De Methodo maximorum & minimorum ad lineas curvas inveniendas applicata in genere.

DEFINITIO I.

ETHODUS maximorum & minimorum ad lineas curvas applicata, est methodus inveniendi lineas curvas, quæ maximi minimive proprietate quapiam propositæ gaudeant.

COROLLARIUM I.

2. Reperiuntur igitur per hanc methodum lineæ curvæ, in quibus proposita quæpiam quantitas maximum vel minimum obtineat valorem.

Euler *De Max. & Min.* A Co-

In his 1740 treatise, *Methodus inveniendi lineas curvas maximi minimive proprietate gaudentes* (Method for finding curved lines enjoying maximum and minimum properties), Euler introduced the calculus of variations. *(Library of Congress)*

Euler wrote several books that provided solid mathematical bases for concepts from diverse areas of science and applied mathematics. In 1744, he published some fundamental results about the calculation of orbits in *Theoria motuum planetarum et cometarum* (Theory of motion of planets and comets). In 1745, he translated Benjamin Robins's *New Principles of Gunnery* and added lengthy supplements on ballistics that became more popular than the original book itself. His *Theoria motus lunae* (Theory of lunar motion) published in 1753 presented detailed mathematical explanations of the motion of the Moon. His book *Theoria motus corporum solidorum seu rigidorum* (Theory of motion of solid rigid bodies) published in 1765 explained the motion of objects as a combination of linear and rotational components.

During this same period of years, Euler wrote several influential books on pure mathematical theory. His *Methodus inveniendi lineas curvas maximi minimive proprietate gaudentes* (Method for finding curved lines enjoying maximum and minimum properties) published in 1740 introduced the branch of mathematics known as the calculus of variations. Other mathematicians described it as one of the most beautiful mathematical works ever written. In 1748, he wrote an influential two-volume book entitled *Introductio in analysin infinitorum* (Introduction to the analysis of the infinite), in which he gave the first formal definition of the concept of a function. He introduced the notation $f(x)$ to represent the function f of x, investigated complex numbers, and introduced the equation that has become known as Euler's identity: $e^{ix} = \cos(x) + i \sin(x)$. When $x = \pi$, this identity produces the famous Euler equation: $e^{i\pi} = -1$. In this book, he redefined calculus as the theory of functions rather than the study of the geometry of curves. His 1755 book, *Institutiones calculi differentialis* (Foundations of differential calculus), presented calculus from the perspective of finite differences.

In 1752, Euler discovered his "edges-plus-two" formula about the geometry of three-dimensional objects called polyhedra. These are objects such as boxes, pyramids, or soccer balls whose sides are polygons—rectangles, triangles, hexagons, and so forth. He discovered that for such objects, the number of faces (or sides) plus the number of vertices (the points where the edges meet) will always equal the number of edges plus 2, or in mathematical notation, $F + V = E + 2$. For a box that has six faces, eight vertices, and 12 edges, the formula gives $6 + 8 = 12 + 2$. For a pyramid with a square base, there are five faces, five vertices, and eight edges, so the formula gives $5 + 5 = 8 + 2$.

One of Euler's projects while in Berlin was to tutor Princess Anhalt Dessau, the king's neice, by writing letters about concepts in light, sound, magnetism, gravity, logic, philosophy, and astronomy. He explained the scientific basis for many physical phenomena, including why it is cold on a mountaintop near the equator, why the Moon looks bigger when it is near the horizon, why the sky is blue, and how the human eye works. A collection of 234 of his letters

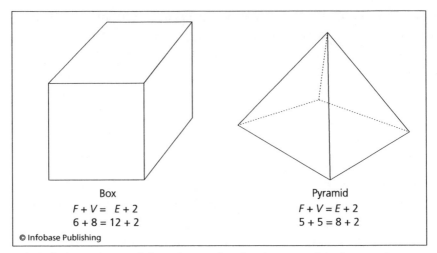

Box
$$F + V = E + 2$$
$$6 + 8 = 12 + 2$$

Pyramid
$$F + V = E + 2$$
$$5 + 5 = 8 + 2$$

© Infobase Publishing

Euler's "edges-plus-two" formula specifies that for any polyhedron, such as a box or a pyramid, the number of faces plus the number of vertices will equal the number of edges plus 2.

to the princess were eventually published between 1768 and 1772 in three volumes under the title *Briefe an eine deutsche Prinzessin* (*Letters to a German Princess*). One of the first examples of popular science written for the nonspecialist, these highly successful books were translated from the original German into English, Russian, Dutch, Swedish, Italian, Spanish, and Danish and were widely sold throughout Europe and the American colonies.

During his years at the Berlin academy, Euler continued to work as the editor of the St. Petersburg math journal and published many of his mathematical discoveries in it. He used his salary as journal editor to buy books and scientific instruments that he sent back to Russia as donations to St. Petersburg Academy. He remained friendly with his colleagues in Russia even when the two countries fought on opposite sides during the Seven Years' War from 1756 to 1763.

In the mid-1760s, King Fredrick the Great began searching for new leadership for the Berlin academy. Even though Euler had brought international fame to the mathematics department during his 25 years at the academy, the king sought to replace him by a more cultured intellectual who had less conservative tastes. Meanwhile, in Russia, a new ruler, Catherine the Great, had come into power and stabilized the political and economic uncertainties in that country. When Euler's colleagues invited him to return to St. Petersburg Academy in 1766, he accepted their invitation.

Return to St. Petersburg Academy, 1766–1783

Euler's first seven years back in St. Petersburg were marked by tragedies. He started to lose the sight in his other eye, and by 1770, he was completely blind. When his house burned to the ground in 1771, he barely escaped with his life and a small number of his mathematical papers. In 1773, Katharina, his wife of 40 years, died.

No longer able to read or write, Euler arranged for other math professors to read books and journal articles to him, describing the diagrams and the graphs as well. These assistants included his son Johann Albrecht Euler, who was the head of the academy's physics department. Euler absorbed the ideas that were read to him, imagined the concepts in his head, and mentally performed the necessary mathematical calculations. When he finished solving a problem or proving a theorem, he dictated his work to the other professors. Using this system, Euler wrote 400 books and papers—50 of them in a single year.

The books he wrote during this period covered a wide range of areas within mathematics and the sciences. To complement his earlier work on differential calculus, he wrote three volumes on integral calculus and differential equations titled *Institutiones calculi integralis* (Foundations of integral calculus) that were published between 1768 and 1770. His three volumes on the optical principles of refracted light rays titled *Dioptrica* (Dioptrics) were published between 1769 and 1771. His algebra textbook titled *Vollständige Anleitung zur Algebra* (Complete guide to algebra) was published in 1770. In 1772, he updated his previous book, in which he mathematically analyzed the motion of the Moon, by publishing a massive 775-page book titled *Theoria motuum lunae, nova methodo pertractata* (Theory of lunar motion, thoroughly treated by a new method). In 1773, he wrote a manual about constructing and maneuvering ships titled *Scientia navalis—Theorie complete de la construction et de la manoeuvre des vaisseaux* (Scientific navigation—complete theory on the construction and maneuvering of vessels) that was adopted by the naval officers' training schools in France and Russia.

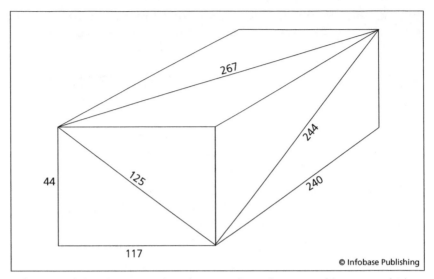

Euler proved that there are infinitely many three-dimensional boxes on which the edges and the diagonals of the six rectangular faces all had integer lengths. Performing the necessary computations in his head, he determined that these dimensions produced the smallest "Euler brick."

Among the new ideas that Euler introduced was the concept of a Euler brick—a three-dimensional box on which the edges and the diagonals of the six rectangular faces all had integer lengths. He proved that there were infinitely many such bricks and that the one with the smallest measurements had edges of lengths 240, 117, and 44, with diagonals of lengths 267, 244, and 125. The skills in mental calculations that he started to develop as a boy enabled him to perform in his head the computations required for this project.

Euler remained active until the last day of his life. On September 18, 1783, after playing with his grandchildren, discussing the mathematics of hot-air ballooning, and making some calculations about the orbit of the planet Uranus, he suffered a massive brain hemorrhage and died at his home in St. Petersburg at the age of 76.

Conclusion

During his lifetime, Euler published 560 books and papers. In the 80 years after his death, his mathematical colleagues published another 300 of his research papers; most of them appeared in the journal of St. Petersburg Academy that he had edited for many years. Three hundred letters that he wrote to other mathematicians and scientists discussing some of his new discoveries have never been published. The collection of all his published works, titled *Opera Omnia* (Complete works), fills 72 volumes—29 volumes on mathematics, 31 on mechanics and astronomy, and 12 on physics and other applied subjects.

Through his prolific writing, Euler influenced not only the mathematical and scientific subject matter but also the form in which it was presented and discussed. He introduced many symbols that have become standard mathematical notation, including e for the natural constant whose value is approximately 2.71828, i for the imaginary number $\sqrt{-1}$, $\sum$ for summations, π for the circle constant whose value is approximately 3.14159, and Δy for the change in the quantity y. Mathematicians have adopted and continue to use so many of the terms, notations, and symbols that he introduced that mathematics after the time of Euler looks dramatically different and much more familiar than the mathematics that was written before his time.

Euler's lifetime of work had a significant influence on trigonometry, calculus, number theory, and many other developing areas of mathematics. His discoveries and theories helped to lay the foundations of new branches of mathematics, including the calculus of variations, differential equations, complex function theory, graph theory, ring theory, and the theory of special functions. His work with applications of mathematics made important contributions to mechanics, astronomy, optics, navigation, physics, ballistics, and insurance. He was so influential in the European mathematical community of his era that mathematicians often refer to the 18th century as the Age of Euler.

FURTHER READING

Dunham, William. *Euler: The Master of Us All*. Washington, D.C.: Mathematical Association of America, 1999. Biography plus chapters about Euler's contributions to many branches of mathematics.

O'Connor, J. J., and E. F. Robertson. "Leonhard Euler," MacTutor History of Mathematics Archive, University of Saint Andrews.

Available online. URL: http://www-groups.dcs.st-andrews. ac.uk/~history/Mathematicians/Euler.html. Accessed March 8, 2004. Online biography, from the University of Saint Andrews, Scotland.

Reimer, Luetta, and Wilbert Reimer. "The Blind Man Who Could See: Leonhard Euler." In *Mathematicians Are People, Too: Stories from the Lives of Great Mathematicians*, 72–81. Parsippany, N.J.: Seymour, 1990. Life story with historical facts and fictionalized dialogue; intended for elementary school students.

Youschkevitch, A. P. "Euler, Leonhard." In *Dictionary of Scientific Biography*, vol. 4, edited by Charles C. Gillispie, 467–484. New York: Scribner, 1972. Detailed encyclopedic biography.

Maria Agnesi

(1718–1799)

Maria Agnesi used her ability to read seven languages to write a calculus textbook that incorporated the discoveries made in all European countries. *(Library of Congress)*

Mathematical Linguist

Maria Gaetana Agnesi (pronounced ahn-YAY-zee) combined her ability to read seven languages with her extensive mathematical talents and wrote a textbook that presented a uniform treatment of calculus. The successful product of 10 years of work earned her high praise from the international mathematical community. She is best remembered for a curve that was mistakenly called "the witch." At the height of her career, she gave up mathematics to devote her life to caring for poor, elderly women.

Early Family Life

Maria Agnesi was born in Milan, Italy, on May 16, 1718, to Don Pietro Agnesi Mariana, an affluent businessman whose family had become wealthy in the profitable silk trade. Maria was the oldest of the 21 Agnesi children from her father's three marriages. Anna Fortunato Brivio Agnesi, her mother, gave birth to eight children and died when Maria was 14 years old.

Maria's father hired a series of distinguished tutors to teach a broad range of subjects to both his sons and his daughters. These instructors included four individuals who were highly trained in mathematics: Michele Casati, a female tutor who later became a professor at the University of Turin; Francesco Manara, who became a professor at the University of Pavia; Carlo Belloni, a prominent mathematician; and Fr. Ramiro Rampinelli, a Catholic priest who had been a professor of mathematics at universities in Rome and Bologna.

As a young girl, Maria demonstrated a talent for learning languages. By the age of five, she spoke fluent French. When she was nine, she translated from Italian into Latin an essay written by one of her tutors advocating higher education for women. Her father paid to publish this essay, titled "Oratio qua ostenditur artium liberalium studia femineo sexu neutiquam abhorrere" (Oration in which it is shown that the study of the liberal arts by the feminine sex is in no way to be despised). By the time she was 11, she could speak, read, and write in seven languages—French, Latin, Greek, Hebrew, German, Spanish, and her native Italian.

A cultured nobleman and a scholar, Mr. Agnesi made his home a center for the exchange of intellectual ideas. He frequently entertained groups of friends, businessmen, and visiting dignitaries at formal dinner parties where Maria would recite speeches in Latin and her sister Maria Teresa would play classical music on the harpsichord. As they grew older, Maria Teresa played musical compositions that she had composed, while Maria engaged in debates with her father's learned guests or read essays that expressed her ideas on political, social, philosophical, or scientific issues of the day. In 1738, her father paid to publish a collection of 191 of her essays as a book titled *Propositiones philosophicae* (Philosophical propositions).

The wide range of topics included philosophy, natural science, logic, ontology, mechanics, elasticity, chemistry, botany, zoology, mineralogy, and the education of women.

Two years earlier, under Rampinelli's guidance, Maria had written a manuscript in which she reviewed two mathematics books—*Traité analytique des sections coniques* (Analytic treatise on conic sections), written in 1707 by Guillaume-François-Antoine, marquis de l'Hôpital, and *Analyse démontré* (Analysis demonstrated), written in 1708 by Charles René Reyneau. L'Hôpital's book discussed the mathematics of conic sections—the curves called circles, ellipses, parabolas, and hyperbolas that described the rotation of a wheel, the orbits of planets, the path of a thrown ball, and the shape of magnifying lenses. Reyneau's calculus book attempted to provide a unified treatment of a collection of mathematical discoveries from the 17th century, including ballistics and planetary motion. Although her work was never published, the mathematicians who reviewed it judged it to be an insightful, accurate, and accessible review of the two mathematical works.

When she was 20 years old, Maria informed her father that she intended to join a convent, where she could become a religious sister and serve the poor. A life of prayer, quiet study, and works of mercy was more attractive to her than debating with dinner guests; attending the opera, the symphony, and the theater; and dressing in formal ball gowns. Her father persuaded her to remain at home, where she could help to educate and raise her younger brothers and sisters. In return, he would excuse her from attending formal social events, allow her to dress simply, and give her time to pray and study.

Instituzioni Analitiche (Analytical Institutions)

For the next 10 years, Agnesi devoted her time to writing a calculus textbook. She originally intended to create for her own enrichment a comprehensive treatment of mathematical analysis similar to l'Hôpital's and Reyneau's books. As she assumed greater responsibility for the education of her brothers and sisters, she redirected the focus of her project to writing a book that they could use in their studies. With Rampinelli's encouragement, the project evolved into a textbook for students at Italian universities that she titled *Instituzioni analitiche ad uso della gioventu italiana* (Analytical institutions for the use of Italian youth).

In this book, Agnesi provided a unified treatment of the concepts of calculus. During the past 100 years, Sir Isaac Newton in England, Gottfried Leibniz in Germany, and mathematicians in France, Russia, Italy, and other European countries had developed different aspects of calculus. They wrote in different languages, invented varied names for the same concepts, and used various notations to represent and manipulate the same ideas. Agnesi used her linguistic and mathematical abilities to translate their work into Italian and to present their results in a uniform manner using Leibniz's differential notation. She presented the material in a natural order so that each idea followed in a logical way from the ideas that came before it. She illustrated theoretical concepts with good examples.

Agnesi became totally absorbed with all aspects of the book's production. On several occasions, after leaving unsolved problems on her desk at the end of the day, she arose from her bed, wrote down the solutions, and returned to bed without waking from her sleep. She made arrangements with a local printer to have a printing press delivered to her family's home so that she could personally supervise every aspect of the printing. To make the book easy to read, she chose to use large pages with wide margins around the edges, selected a large size print, and included a generous collection of diagrams and illustrations. Italian mathematician Jacopo Riccati read early drafts of her work, recommended revisions, and shared with her some of his unpublished work on integration.

After 10 years of work, Agnesi published her book—the first volume in 1748 and the second a year later. The massive project comprised 1,020 pages of text, a page of corrections, and a 49-page appendix of illustrations—a set of oversize pages that could be opened outward, enabling the reader to view the figures while also reading the text. The first volume presented analysis of finite quantities including elementary algebra, the classical theory of equations, coordinate geometry, the construction of conic sections, and techniques from analytic geometry for finding maxima, minima, tangents, and points of inflection. The second volume, organized into three sections each with several chapters, presented the analysis of infinitesimally small quantities. The topics included differential calculus, integral calculus, power series, the inverse method of tangents, and the fundamentals of differential equations.

Reactions to the Book

Instituzioni analitiche was a major achievement that attracted international attention and brought Agnesi recognition as a mathematician. The book won immediate acclaim in academic circles as the first comprehensive textbook on calculus since l'Hôpital's 1696 work, *Analyse des infiniment petits* (Analysis of the infinitely small). A committee of mathematicians headed by Jean d'Ortous de Mairan and Étienne Mignot de Montigny at the French Academy of Sciences praised Agnesi for skillfully combining the work of various mathematicians into an accessible and comprehensive book. They commended her for the book's clarity, orderliness, and precision, describing it as the most complete and clearly written text available on the subject in any language.

Agnesi dedicated the book to Maria Theresa, the empress of Austria and ruler of the Hapsburg Empire that included the northern region of Italy where Agnesi lived. In the first pages of the book, Agnesi wrote that Maria Theresa was her role model and had been her inspiration throughout the course of her work. The empress, honored by the dedication and impressed by the achievement of a woman mathematician, sent her a diamond ring and an ornate crystal box decorated with gems and diamonds.

Pope Benedict XIV wrote to Agnesi, congratulating her on the credit that her achievement brought to Italy, and presented her with a gold medal and a gold wreath decorated with precious gemstones. In 1750, on the recommendation of the president of the University of Bologna and several members of the Italian Academy of Sciences, the pope offered her an appointment as chair of mathematics and natural philosophy at the University of Bologna. Although the university sent her a diploma as an official confirmation of the appointment and listed her name as a member of the faculty for the next 45 years, historical sources indicate that she never went to the university or taught any classes there. The Bologna Academy of Sciences elected Agnesi as a one of its first female members.

In the same year that the first volume of Agnesi's book appeared, Swiss mathematician Leonhard Euler published a calculus text titled *Introductio in analysin infinitorum* (Introduction to the analysis of the infinite). This classic text, along with his *Institutiones calculi differentialis* (Foundations of differential calculus) that appeared seven years later, overshadowed Agnesi's work as the definitive treatment of the subject. Despite competition from these and other works, her book was translated into many languages and remained a popular textbook in many European countries for 60 years. In 1775, when the members of the French Academy of Sciences wanted to prepare an elementary calculus textbook that would include recent discoveries in trigonometry, they authorized Pierre Thomas Antelmy to translate the second volume of Agnesi's book into French, add additional material on trigonometry, and publish it under the title *Traités élémentaires de calcul* (Elementary treatise of calculus). New editions of her work continued to appear into the 19th century. The most well known of these was John Colson's English translation, completed before his death in 1760 but not published until 1801 under the title *Analytical institutions.*

"The Witch of Agnesi"

One particular example that Agnesi included near the end of the first volume of her book attracted much attention after the publication of Colson's translation of the work. The example was a cubic curve—a curve in whose equation the highest-degree term had an exponent of three—that is sometimes called a versed sine curve. Other mathematicians had studied this curve in the previous century. In 1665, French mathematician Pierre de Fermat had written about the equation of this curve. In 1703, Italian mathematician Guido Grandi had provided a detailed description of the construction of its graph. Grandi had given the curve the name *versoria* from the Latin verb *vertere*, meaning "to turn." Agnesi used the Italian word *versiera* as the name of the curve.

Colson, a professor at Cambridge University in England, learned to read Italian in order to be able to translate Agnesi's work into

English. When he attempted to translate the name of this cubic curve, he confused *la versiera* with *l'avversiera*, meaning "the wife of the devil" or "the woman who was against God," and translated the name of the curve as "the witch." Although other translators had called the curve the cubic of Agnesi or the Agnesienne, Colson's mistake was quite memorable, and in the English-speaking world, the curve became popularly known as "the witch of Agnesi."

The equation of the curve is $y = \dfrac{a^3}{x^2 + a^2}$. For any fixed value of a, the set of points whose coordinates (x, y) satisfy this equation describe a curve that flows down both sides of a circle, leveling out as it spreads away from the circle. The curve can be constructed by sketching the circle of radius a centered at the point $(0, a)$ and the two horizontal lines $y = 0$ and $y = 2a$ that are tangent to it at the points $(0, 0)$ and $(0, 2a)$, respectively. Each straight line drawn through the origin $(0, 0)$ will intersect the circle at some point (b, c) and will intersect the line $y = 2a$ at some point $(d, 2a)$. For each such line, the point (d, c) will be a point on the curve. By drawing many lines through the point $(0, 0)$ with different slopes, one can produce a collection of points that form the curve. The resulting curve has many interesting mathematical properties, including a local maximum, two points of inflections, left-right symmetry, and a horizontal asymptote.

Agnesi presented this curve in four places in her textbook. Near the end of the introductory volume, she used it as an exercise in

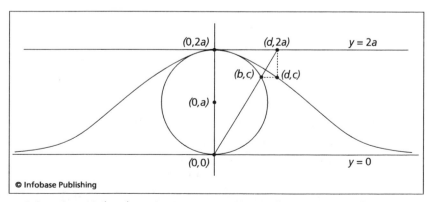

Each line through (o, o) produces one point on the "witch of Agnesi" curve.

analytic geometry when she described the curve geometrically and asked the reader to find its equation. She illustrated the construction of the graph in the set of diagrams that folded out from the back of the book. At the very end of the first volume, she presented an algebraic method for finding the curve's points of inflection. In the second volume, she revisited the curve when she had developed a more sophisticated technique for finding points of inflection by the method of second derivatives. Although Agnesi did not offer any applications of the curve, physicists in the 1940s discovered that the curve approximates the spectral energy distribution of X-ray lines and optical lines as well as the power dissipated in sharply tuned resonant circuits.

Second Career after Mathematics

When her father died in 1752, Agnesi embraced the opportunity to devote her life to the service of the poor. Although the success of her textbook had established her reputation within the Italian mathematical community and brought her recognition throughout Europe, she abruptly discontinued her work in mathematics. No longer needed to help raise her brothers and sisters, she devoted the next 47 years of her life to the care of poor, elderly women. Initially, she used several rooms in her family's home to care for and comfort her patients. In 1759, she sold the gold medal that the pope had given to her and the diamond and crystal box Empress Maria Theresa had presented to her. She used the money to set up a nursing home in a rented building in Milan.

Despite her retirement from the world of mathematics, other mathematicians maintained a high opinion of her abilities. In 1762, professors from the University of Turin wrote to Agnesi, asking her to review a paper that announced some new discoveries in the calculus of variations. The paper's author, Joseph Louis Lagrange, was a young mathematician who eventually became one of the greatest mathematicians of his era. Agnesi declined the request, explaining that she no longer did any mathematics.

In 1771, at the request of Archbishop Tozzobonelli, Agnesi became the director of Pio Albergo Trivulzio, a nursing home for poor women. The facility had been the palace of Prince Antonio

Tolemeo Trivulzio, who had donated it to the church to be used as a home for the aged. As she had done with her mathematics, Agnesi became totally absorbed in her work as the administrator responsible for the care of the facility's 450 patients. In 1783, she took up residence in the nursing home to be closer to the women she served.

After more than 40 years of caring for poor women, Agnesi's health failed. For the last five years of her life, she was a patient in the nursing home that she had run. She grew blind and deaf, had fainting spells, and suffered from dropsy. She died penniless at Pio Albergo Trivulzio on January 9, 1799, at the age of 80. She was buried in an unmarked grave with 15 other women who had been patients at the nursing home.

Conclusion

On the 100th anniversary of her death, the citizens of Milan, Monza, and Masciago honored Agnesi by naming streets after her. In Milan, a school for teachers was named after her, and scholarships for girls have been established in her name. An engraved cornerstone at the nursing home recalls her service to poor women.

Agnesi's calculus book, *Instituzioni analitiche*, was one of the most important mathematical publications produced by a woman before the mid-18th century. It represented one of the first successful attempts to present a unified treatment of the fundamentals of calculus. In this work, she combined the research results that had been produced by the early developers of calculus and had been published in several different languages using a variety of notations and presented them in a single language with consistent terminology and notation. This widely used textbook remains the oldest-surviving mathematical work written by a woman. Although her name has been most closely associated with the curve that has come to be known as "the witch of Agnesi," the mathematical community has recently developed an interest in the wider body of her work.

FURTHER READING

Gray, Shirley B. "Maria Gaetana Agnesi," California State University, Los Angeles. Available online. URL: http://instructional1.cal

statela.edu/sgray/agnesi. Accessed March 14, 2003. Web site established by Professor Gray that is devoted to Agnesi; includes many photos.

————, and Tagui Malalyan. "The Witch of Agnesi—A Lasting Contribution from the First Surviving Mathematical Work Written by a Woman." *College Mathematics Journal* 30, no. 4 (1999): 258–268. Unique journal article with many illustrations.

Kramer, Edna E. "Agnesi, Maria Gaetana." In *Dictionary of Scientific Biography*, vol. 1, edited by Charles C. Gillispie, 75–77. New York: Scribner, 1972. Encyclopedic biography.

O'Connor, J. J., and E. F. Robertson. "Maria Gaëtana Agnesi," MacTutor History of Mathematics Archive, University of Saint Andrews. Available online. URL: http://www-groups.dcs.st-andrews.ac.uk/~history/Mathematicians/Agnesi.html. Accessed March 14, 2003. Online biography, from the University of Saint Andrews, Scotland.

Osen, Lynn M. "The 'Witch' of Agnesi." In *Women in Mathematics*, 33–48. Cambridge, Mass.: MIT Press, 1974. Detailed biography.

Perl, Teri. "Maria Gaetana Agnesi." In *Math Equals: Biographies of Women Mathematicians and Related Activities*, 53–61. Menlo Park, Calif.: Addison-Wesley, 1978. Detailed biography accompanied by exercises related to her mathematical work.

Reimer, Luetta, and Wilbert Reimer. "The Gift of Sympathy: Maria Agnesi." In *Mathematicians Are People, Too: Stories from the Lives of Great Mathematicians*, vol. 2, 52–79. Parsippany, N.J.: Seymour, 1995. Life story with historical facts and fictionalized dialogue; intended for elementary school students.

Benjamin Banneker

(1731–1806)

Benjamin Banneker, a self-taught African-American tobacco farmer, helped to survey the boundaries of the District of Columbia and calculated the astronomical and tidal data for 12 almanacs. *(The Granger Collection)*

Early African-American Scientist

Benjamin Banneker was an African-American tobacco farmer in colonial America who used his free time to pursue his interest in mathematics. As a young man, he demonstrated advanced geometrical insight when he designed and built a wooden clock. At the age of 57, with borrowed books and equipment, he taught himself the mathematical principles of astronomy. With this knowledge, he helped to survey the boundaries of the District of Columbia. For 12 years, he calculated annual almanacs for the farmers and sailors of Maryland and neighboring states. These achievements made him an international figure in the antislavery movement of his day.

Tobacco Farmer

Benjamin Banneker was born on November 9, 1731, at his grandparents' tobacco farm outside of Baltimore, Maryland. He was a free man in a family that had experienced two generations of slavery. In 1683, his grandmother Molly Welsh was sent from an English dairy farm, where she was accused of stealing milk, to a Maryland tobacco farm, where she worked for seven years as an indentured servant. After completing her period of service, she bought a small farm in rural Baltimore County and two African slaves whom she freed after four years. In 1696, Welsh married her former slave Bannaka, and the two took the name Banneky as their family name. In 1730, their oldest daughter, Mary, married a former African slave named Robert and kept the family name Banneky. A year later, Benjamin, the first of their four children, was born. He later changed his name to Banneker.

Banneker's education was limited by his isolation on a rural farm and by the demands of an agricultural life. In 1737, Robert and Mary Banneky bought a 100-acre farm in present-day Oella, Maryland, where Banneker lived the rest of his life in the one-room log cabin that his father built. Tobacco farming required long hours of difficult work each day, leaving little time for relaxation or for education. When he was a child with few responsibilities, Banneker's Grandmother Welsh taught him to read and write, and for a few months each winter, he attended a local schoolhouse where he studied arithmetic, history, and other subjects. His limited formal education lasted only until he became old enough to work full time on the farm, but throughout his life, he continued to read books, pamphlets, and newspapers; enjoyed solving number puzzles; and learned to play the fiddle and the flute.

Wooden Clock

At the age of 22, Banneker had the opportunity to examine the inner workings of a pocket watch—a rare and expensive possession at the time. After studying the intricate coordination of the gears and springs, he sketched the design of a clock that would display the hours and minutes with its hands and strike a chime at the beginning of every hour. He carved the gears and other parts of the clock from pieces of wood, assembled his homemade device, and mounted his unique timepiece on the wall of his family's cabin, where it accurately kept time for the next 52 years.

In the American colonies in the 1750s, the few craftsmen who made timepieces were highly trained through years of work as apprentices to master clockmakers in well-equipped workshops with specialized tools and materials. For an amateur who had only seen the workings of one timepiece, to understand the geometrical relationships between the many gears and springs well enough to design and build a reliable timepiece was a remarkable achievement. Banneker's wooden clock made him a local celebrity and attracted curious visitors to his rural farm.

Diverse Interests

Banneker's father died in 1759, leaving him to care for his mother and to run the family's farm. In addition to these demands on his time, he maintained his interests in music, reading, mathematics, science, and current events. As one of the few literate individuals in the area, he helped his neighboring farmers to make calculations, write letters, and read formal correspondence. In a journal, he recorded his observations of the 17-year cycles of the locusts and the intricate flights of his honeybees. One of the mathematical puzzles he noted in his journal asked the solver to find four numbers that added up to 60 and also had the property that the first number plus 4, the second number minus 4, the third number times 4, and the fourth number divided by 4 were all equal. Although he did not create this puzzle, his fascination with these mathematical recreations demonstrated his sustained interest in mathematics and his well-developed mathematical abilities.

In 1771, five brothers named Ellicott purchased land along the nearby Patapsco River and constructed two mills for grinding wheat into flour. They built homes for their families, boardinghouses for their mill workers, a general store, and a meetinghouse. Banneker

Problem: Determine the values of a, b, c, and d so that

$$a + b + c + d = 60$$

$$a + 4 = b - 4 = c \times 4 = d \div 4$$

Answer: $a = 5.6$, $b = 13.6$, $c = 2.4$, $d = 38.4$

One of the arithmetic puzzles Banneker recorded in his mathematical journal.

spent many hours visiting with his neighbors, discussing politics, reading newspapers, and observing the operation of their mills. He eventually became close friends with one of their sons, George Ellicott. Although Ellicott was 29 years younger than Banneker, the two shared common interests in mathematics and science.

Astronomer

After his mother died in the late 1770s, Banneker gradually scaled back on his farming and devoted more time to his other interests. In 1788, George Ellicott lent him four books on astronomy, some astronomical instruments, and a telescope. The books included James Ferguson's *An Easy Introduction to Astronomy* and Charles Leadbetter's *A Compleat System of Astronomy*. Within months, he learned how to calculate the times of sunrise and sunset, how to predict when the Moon would rise and set each night, and how to determine when it would pass through its phases from new moon to full moon and back again. He learned how to determine the dates of eclipses that take place three or four times each year when the Moon disappears as it passes into the shadow cast by the Earth (lunar eclipse) or the Sun disappears as the Earth passes into the shadow cast by the Moon (solar eclipse).

After several months of study and practice, Banneker showed his calculations for the prediction of a solar eclipse to Ellicott, who discovered only one mistake. To predict an eclipse, an astronomer needed to make 36 calculations and a series of precise geometrical drawings. In his sequence of computations, Banneker confused the details of two different methods that had been presented in the

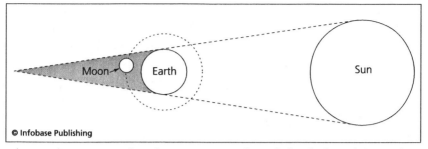

A lunar eclipse occurs when the Moon passes through the shadow of the Earth.

books by Ferguson and Leadbetter. He revised his calculations and correctly predicted the solar eclipse for April 14, 1789. Impressed with Banneker's rapid mastery of the techniques of astronomy, Ellicott encouraged him to write an almanac.

In the 18th century, an almanac was one of the few printed publications that a typical American family owned. These inexpensive pamphlets of 20 to 30 pages provided valuable information and entertaining reading material. Ships' captains relied on almanacs for listings of high and low tides to help them determine the best times for setting sail and for navigating shallow coastal waterways. Sailors depended on almanacs to provide them with the positions of the stars so they could accurately determine their location on the open sea. Farmers planted and harvested according to the phases of the Moon that were listed in the almanacs and relied on weather predictions and the reported times of sunrise and sunset to plan their daily activities. Almanacs also served as calendars, listing dates of important events such as holidays, fairs, and traveling courts. Two of the best-known almanacs were *Poor Richard's Almanac*, which was produced in Philadelphia by Benjamin Franklin for 25 years, and *The Farmer's Almanac*, which continues to be published today.

The daily listing of the times and positions of the Sun, Moon, planets, and stars was called an ephemeris. The substantial abilities of a skilled astronomer were required to make the thousands of calculations and measurements necessary to produce accurate data for an ephemeris. Calculating the times of high and low tides were relatively simple procedures because these events occurred on a regular basis, with a new high tide approximately every 12 hours and 25 minutes. Determining the timing of events that happened in the sky was more complicated. As the Earth orbits the Sun and spins on its axis, it also wobbles slightly. The orbit of the Moon around the Earth varies as much as five degrees above and below the plane defined by the Earth's equator. The arrangement of heavenly bodies appears different to observers only a few hundred miles apart from each other, so the astronomical calculations produced for farmers in Maryland were of no use to a person in New York or Atlanta.

Banneker devoted all his available time to making the calculations for an almanac for 1791. When he completed his work, he sent packets containing his neatly organized pages to three printers in Baltimore. Before a printer would agree to publish an almanac, he would usually ask an established astronomer to review the calculations for accuracy. Printer John Hayes sent Banneker's almanac to George Ellicott's cousin Andrew Ellicott, a well-known engineer and astronomer who had published almanacs for each of the previous 10 years. Andrew Ellicott reviewed Banneker's calculations and found them to be reasonably accurate. Despite this positive evaluation, Hayes decided not to publish Banneker's almanac. Since it was too late in the year to make arrangements with another printer, his 1791 almanac was never published. Although this unsuccessful venture disappointed Banneker, he resolved to produce an almanac for 1792, taking care to make more accurate calculations and to secure a printer earlier in the year.

Surveying the District of Columbia

Before he could make much progress on the 1792 almanac, Banneker was offered another opportunity to utilize his talents in astronomy. Since 1776, when America declared its independence from England, Congress had met in eight different locations because the country did not have a permanent capital city. In 1790, President George Washington and Congress approved the creation of a 100-square-mile federal territory to be known as the District of Columbia, located on the boundary of Virginia and Maryland. Secretary of State Thomas Jefferson appointed Andrew Ellicott to direct a team of surveyors who would measure and mark the boundaries of the square plot of land—10 miles on each side—where the capital city would be built.

Ellicott's brothers, who had helped him to survey the boundaries of Pennsylvania and Virginia, were unable to leave their current project surveying the western boundary of New York State. He needed someone who possessed knowledge of astronomy, who was capable of taking careful measurements with astronomical equipment, and who could make complicated mathematical calculations. When his cousin George Ellicott recommended that he hire Banneker, he recalled the impressive work Banneker had done for his almanac and offered him the position. The self-taught 59-year-old amateur astronomer and almanac-maker who had never been more than a few miles from his farm accepted the offer.

Although the project was noble, the working conditions were harsh. Banneker spent the months of February, March, and April living in a cold tent in the woods of Maryland and Virginia. His primary responsibility was to maintain the astronomical clock, a complicated and sensitive device that was affected by changes in temperature, moderate vibrations, and accidental contact. By accurately coordinating the clock's time with the predictable movements of the stars and other heavenly bodies, this instrument enabled the surveying team to determine their precise latitude and longitude as well as the exact direction of true north. Banneker's responsibilities required him to stay awake for most of the night observing and recording the locations of stars, the Moon, and the planets. He rested during the afternoons between observations of the Sun and other stars that were visible during the day through Ellicott's powerful telescope. The reliability of his observations and the accuracy of his calculations were important to the success of the survey. A small error in the measurement of an angle extended over a distance of 10 miles would produce very inaccurate results.

The eight-man team completed their three-month project laying out the boundaries of the 10-mile square with acceptable precision. The four sides of the square were each within 263 feet of 10 miles, an error of less than one-half of 1 percent. The plans called for the northernmost corner of the square plot of land to be due north from the southernmost corner. The line passing through the two corners marked by the surveying team was within $1/_{12}$th of a degree of being true north. While Ellicott, French engineer Pierre Charles L'Enfant, and others moved on to the next phase of the project—laying out the streets of the city that would become Washington, D.C.—Banneker returned to his farm.

1792 Almanac

Banneker immediately began to work on his almanac for the year 1792. Having learned the importance of organization and precision, he carefully recorded his astronomical observations in a large book and double checked each calculation. His experience of working with Ellicott's advanced equipment and of making lengthy calculations with great accuracy helped to speed his progress on this project. Early in June 1791, he finished all the necessary calculations, prepared his almanac, and sent it to printers in Baltimore and Georgetown who both agreed to publish it.

The news that an almanac written by an African American would soon be published generated considerable interest, especially among the members of the antislavery movement. At the July meeting of the Maryland Society for Promoting the Abolition of Slavery, George Buchanan, a respected physician and public speaker, praised Banneker's achievements in astronomy along with those of other African-American men and women who had distinguished themselves as writers, poets, and doctors. James Pemberton, the president of the Pennsylvania Society for Promoting the Abolition of Slavery, contacted Banneker to obtain a copy of his almanac and submitted it to recognized astronomers for their critical review. David Rittenhouse, who was the leading astronomer in the country and was president of the American Philosophical Society, and William Waring, who was a well-known teacher, writer, and astronomer who had published five almanacs, both checked Banneker's calculations. They agreed that he had done an excellent job and recommended that the almanac be published. These reviews convinced Philadelphia printer Joseph Crukshank to agree to publish and distribute the almanac as well.

In August 1791, Banneker sent a copy of his almanac to Secretary of State Jefferson with a 12-page letter offering his work on the almanac and on the survey of the District of Columbia as evidence of what African Americans could achieve in scientific fields. Jefferson wrote back, congratulating Banneker for developing his advanced mathematical abilities and praising him for being a credit to his race. Jefferson sent the almanac to the Marquis de Condorcet, the secretary of the French Academy of Sciences, so that his achievements could be known throughout Europe.

In the fall of 1791, the almanac was offered for sale with the full title of *Benjamin Banneker's Pennsylvania, Delaware, Maryland, and Virginia Almanack and Ephemeris, For the Year of Our Lord, 1792; Being Bisextile, or Leap-Year, and the Sixteenth Year of American Independence, which commenced July 4, 1776. Containing, the Motions of the Sun and Moon, the true Places and Aspects of the Planets, the Rising and Setting of the Sun, and the Rising, Setting and Southing, Place and Age of the Moon, etc.—The Lunation, Conjunction, Eclipses, Judgment of the Weather, festivals, and other remarkable Days; Days for holding the Supreme and Circuit Courts of the United States, as also the usual Courts in Pennsylvania, Delaware, Maryland, and Virginia.—Also, Several useful Tables and valuable receipts.—Various Selections from the Commonplace-Book of the Kentucky Philosopher, an American Sage; with interesting and entertaining Essays, in Prose and Verse—the Whole comprising a greater, more pleasing, and useful Variety, than any Work of the Kind and Price in North-America.* Although the printer in Georgetown decided not to publish the almanac, five printers in three cities— Goddard and Angell in Baltimore, Hanson and Bond in Alexandria, Crukshank in Philadelphia, Humphreys in Philadelphia, and Young in Philadelphia—distributed three different versions of the work. The almanac was so popular in Baltimore that Goddard and Angell had to make a second printing. In addition to Banneker's calculations and the collection of items mentioned in its title, the almanac included an introduction written by Maryland senator James McHenry praising the work Banneker had done to create this almanac and to help with the surveying of the District of Columbia. In England, members of the House of Commons presented copies of Banneker's 1792 almanac as evidence of the advanced achievement of an African American in support of the cause of the antislavery movement.

Professional Almanac-Maker

Banneker took the opportunity provided by the success of his almanac to stop raising tobacco and become a professional almanac-maker. The Ellicotts purchased his farm for £180 (the unit of currency at the time) through a reverse mortgage. They agreed to allow him to live on the property until he died and to give him 12 pounds of credit at their general store each year. At the end of the year, they paid him whatever balance they owed to him. Banneker was content that this steady stream of annual income combined with the profits from the sales of his almanacs would enable him to live a simple lifestyle making astronomical observations at night without having to labor on his farm during the day.

The almanac Banneker produced for 1793 was even more successful than his first published one. Crukshank in Philadelphia published it under the title *Banneker's Almanack, and Ephemeris For the Year of our Lord, 1793*. Goddard and Angel in Baltimore published a slightly different version, titled *Benjamin Banneker's Pennsylvania, Maryland and Virginia Almanack and Ephemeris For the Year of our Lord, 1793*. In addition to his astronomical calculations, both versions included Banneker's letter to Secretary of State Jefferson and Jefferson's reply. Crukshank's version also included a letter titled "A Plan of a Peace Office for the United States," written by Quaker doctor Benjamin Rush, one of the signers of the Declaration of Independence, which advocated for the establishment of a peace office in the president's cabinet. The inclusion of these three letters made Banneker's 1793 almanac one of the most important publications in the country that year. Widely discussed at all levels of society, it sold more copies than Andrew Ellicott's almanac for the same year and had to be printed in a second edition after the first printing sold out completely.

From 1792 through 1797, 12 printers in seven cities in New Jersey, Delaware, Maryland, Pennsylvania, and Virginia published 28 editions of Banneker's almanacs. Five of the 14 editions of his highly successful 1795 almanac prominently publicized his ethnicity. The title of the edition printed in Trenton, New Jersey, by Matthias Day included the phrase *The Astronomical Calculations by Benjamin Banneker, An African*. Publishers John Fisher in Baltimore, William Gibbons in Philadelphia, Jacob Johnson in Philadelphia, and Samuel and John Adams in Wilmington, Delaware, featured Banneker's picture on the cover of their editions of the almanac. Although it was not an accurate portrait of Banneker, the engraving

Banneker's portrait appeared on the covers of several editions of his 1795 almanac. *(The Granger Collection)*

depicting an intelligent and dignified African American was one of the earliest-known instances of a publisher using the image of an African-American author for the purpose of increasing the sales of a printed item.

By 1797, the movement to abolish slavery lost its momentum, and the political leaders of America turned their attention to other national issues. Banneker continued to make calculations for almanacs until 1802, but without the support of antislavery organizations, he was unable to get them published. Although he had established a reputation for his accurate astronomical calculations, printers no longer perceived public interest in an almanac created by an African American.

On October 9, 1806, just a month before his 75th birthday, Benjamin Banneker died at his farm. As he had requested before his death, his sisters and nephews returned to George Ellicott the telescope, books, and astronomical instruments that he had loaned to Banneker. They saved the notebooks in which he recorded his astronomical calculations and his mathematical puzzles, but the wooden clock that had been the earliest sign of his mathematical talents burned in a fire that consumed his log cabin on the day of his funeral.

Honors and Memorials

During the two centuries since his death, dozens of biographical sketches in books, journals, and movies have offered Banneker's life as an example of the intellectual capabilities of African Americans. Typical of these was Moncure Conway's 1863 article "Benjamin Banneker, The Negro Astronomer" in the *Atlantic Monthly*, which was reprinted as a pamphlet and widely distributed throughout the northern states and in England in support of the antislavery movement during the Civil War. Among the many biographies of Banneker was one written by George Ellicott's daughter Martha Tyson titled *A Sketch of the Life of Benjamin Banneker; From Notes Taken in 1836*, which her nephew presented to the Maryland Historical Society in 1854 and her daughter published as a book in 1884. Many professional societies, including the National Council of Teachers of Mathematics, the Association for the Study of Afro American Life and History, and the National Association of Watch and Clock Collectors, have published the story of Banneker's life, highlighting those aspects that are most interesting to their members.

Groups of individuals have formed organizations and established institutions to honor Banneker's achievements in mathematics, astronomy, surveying, clock making, and civil rights. In 1853, a group in Philadelphia established the Banneker Institute to provide opportunities for young African-American men to further their education through monthly lectures and debates. Hundreds of schools, institutions, and organizations bearing his name, such as the Benjamin Banneker Center for Economic Justice in Baltimore; the Benjamin Banneker Association in East Lansing, Michigan; and the Banneker-Douglas Museum in Annapolis, Maryland, continue to recognize his exemplary life. In 1985, Baltimore County purchased a large portion of his farm and established the Benjamin Banneker Park and Museum as a historical site.

Banneker's memory and legacy are preserved by recent national honors. In 1980, the United States Postal Service issued a commemorative stamp depicting Banneker surveying the boundaries of Washington, D.C. The National Surveyor's Hall of Fame inducted him in 1996 as one of their 10 charter members along with Andrew Ellicott, David Rittenhouse, George Washington, and Thomas Jefferson. In 1998, President William Jefferson Clinton signed into law legislation to build a Banneker Memorial in Washington, D.C.

Conclusion

At the age of 57, Benjamin Banneker, a colonial American tobacco farmer, taught himself the mathematical principles of astronomy and became an amateur mathematician. He made precise measurements and detailed calculations as a member of the team of surveyors who determined the boundaries of the District of Columbia. For 12 years, he accurately made the thousands of calculations of planetary, lunar, and solar positions that were necessary to produce annual almanacs for the Mid-Atlantic states. His achievements as a self-taught African American earned him international recognition as a prominent figure in the antislavery movement.

FURTHER READING

Bedini, Silvio A. *The Life of Benjamin Banneker: The First African-American Man of Science*. Baltimore: Maryland Historical Society, 1999. Authoritative full-length biography researched from original correspondence and historical documents.

DuBois, Shirley Graham. *Your Most Humble Servant*. New York: Messner, 1949. Full-length biography.

Freedom Man. VHS, 61 minutes. Network Home Entertainment, 1989. Videorecording reenacting significant events in Banneker's life.

O'Connor, J. J., and E. F. Robertson. "Benjamin Banneker," MacTutor History of Mathematics Archive, University of Saint Andrews. Available online. URL: http://www-groups. dcs.st-andrews.ac.uk/~history/Mathematicians/Banneker.html. Accessed January 27, 2003. Online biography, from the University of Saint Andrews, Scotland.

Reimer, Luetta, and Wilbert Reimer. "The Shy Sky Watcher: Benjamin Banneker." In *Mathematicians Are People, Too: Stories from the Lives of Great Mathematicians*, vol. 2, 62–71. Parsippany, N.J.: Seymour, 1995. Life story with historical facts and fictionalized dialogue; intended for elementary school students.

GLOSSARY

alchemy   The practice of attempting to discover a method for converting common chemicals into gold.

algebra   The branch of mathematics dealing with the manipulation of variables and equations.

algebraic expression   An expression built up out of numbers and variables using the operations of addition, subtraction, multiplication, division, raising to a power, and taking a root.

almanac   A pamphlet listing the times of tides and astronomical events along with reading material and a calendar of local events.

amicable numbers   See FRIENDLY NUMBERS.

analytic art   One of several names for algebra in the 17th century. Also known as LOGISTIC ANALYSIS.

analytic geometry   The algebraic study of geometric curves as a collection of points whose coordinates satisfy an associated equation.

angle   A planar figure formed by two rays with a common endpoint.

approximation   An estimate for the value of a numerical quantity.

arc   The portion of the circumference of a circle between two specified points.

Archimedean spiral   A spiral traced out by a point rotating about a fixed point at a constant angular speed while simultaneously moving away from the fixed point at a constant speed. It is given in polar coordinates by $r = a\theta$, where a is a positive constant.

arithmetic   The study of computation.

arithmetic series An infinite sum of the form $a + (a + r) + (a + 2r) + (a + 3r) + \dots$

armillary sphere A three-dimensional model of the universe with movable and stationary rings representing the orbits of the planets and the locations of the stars.

astrolabe A mechanical device used to measure the inclination of a star or other object of observation.

astrology A mystical theory that explains how a person's personality and fate are determined by the positions of the stars and planets at the time he or she was born.

astronomy The study of stars, planets, and other heavenly bodies.

axiom A statement giving a property of an undefined term or a relationship between undefined terms. The axioms of a specific mathematical theory govern the behavior of the undefined terms in that theory; they are assumed to be true and cannot be proved. Also known as a POSTULATE.

axis A line used to measure coordinates in analytic geometry.

binary Base-2.

binary number A number written as a sum of powers of 2.

binomial coefficient A positive integer given by the computation $\binom{n}{k} = \dfrac{n!}{k!(n-k)!}$, where n and k are integers satisfying $0 \le k \le n$.

binomial theorem The general statement that the sum of two quantities raised to any integer or fractional power can be written as a finite or infinite sum of terms using the generalized binomial coefficients according to the formula

$$(a + b)^n = a^n + \binom{n}{1} a^{n-1}b + \binom{n}{2} a^{n-2}b^2 + \binom{n}{3} a^{n-3}b^3 + \dots.$$

bisect To divide into two congruent pieces, as a line segment or a circle.

brachistochrone problem A geometry problem involving the shortest path between two nonvertical points under the force of gravity.

calculus The branch of mathematics dealing with derivatives and integrals.

center of gravity   The point at which a physical object will balance under the force of gravity.

central angle   An angle formed by two radii of the same circle.

chord   A line segment whose two endpoints lie on a circle.

circle   The set of all points in a plane at a given distance (the radius) from a fixed point (the center).

circumference   (1) The points on a circle. (2) The measure of the total arc length of a circle; it is 2π times the radius of the circle.

circumscribed polygon   A polygon, with each edge tangent to the circumference of a circle.

coefficient   A number or known quantity that multiplies a variable in an algebraic expression.

common logarithm   A logarithm that expresses a given quantity as a power of 10.

composite number   A positive integer that can be factored as the product of two or more primes.

cone   The surface swept out by a line that is rotated about an axis while keeping one point (the vertex) fixed.

conic   The curved shapes—ellipse, parabola, and hyperbola—obtained by the intersection of a plane with a cone. Also known as a CONIC SECTION.

conic section   See CONIC.

coordinates   The numbers indicating the location of a point on a plane or in a higher-dimensional space.

cosine   For an acute angle in a right triangle, the ratio of the adjacent side to the hypotenuse.

cube   (1) A regular solid having six congruent faces, each of which is a square. (2) To multiply a quantity times itself three times; raise to the third power.

cubic   A polynomial of degree 3. Also an equation or curve (graph) corresponding to a cubic polynomial.

cycloid   The path traced by a point on a circle as the circle rolls along a straight line. Also known as a ROULETTE.

cylinder   A solid with two congruent bases (usually circles) connected by a lateral surface generated by segments connecting corresponding points on the two bases.

decimal   Base-10.

decimal fraction A fraction whose denominator is a power of 10.

decimal point A dot used to separate the integer and fractional parts of a number written in base-10 notation.

degree (1) A unit of angle measure equal to 1/360 of a circle. (2) The number of edges that meet at a vertex in a polygon or polyhedron. (3) The sum of the exponents of all the variables occurring in a term of a polynomial or algebraic expression.

degree of a polynomial or equation The highest exponent occurring in any of its terms.

derivative A function formed as the limit of a ratio of differences of the values of another function. One of two fundamental ideas of calculus that indicates the rate at which a quantity is changing.

diagonal In a square or a rectangle, the line joining two opposite corners.

diameter (1) The distance across a circle. (2) A line segment of this length passing through the center of a circle joining two points on opposite sides of the circle.

differential equation An equation involving derivatives.

differentiation The process of determining the derivative of a function.

divisible A number is divisible by another if the resulting quotient has no remainder.

eclipse An astronomical event that occurs when the Sun, Earth, and Moon align and either the Moon disappears as it passes into the shadow cast by the Earth (lunar eclipse) or the Sun disappears as the Earth passes into the shadow cast by the Moon (solar eclipse).

ellipse The intersection of a cone with a plane that meets the cone in a closed curve. Equivalently, the set of points whose distances from two fixed points, called the foci of the ellipse, have a constant sum.

encryption The process of translating a message into a secret code.

ephemeris The tables in an almanac that specify the times of the occurrences of celestial events, such as sunrise, sunset, eclipses, and the phases of the Moon.

equation   A mathematical sentence stating that two algebraic expressions or numerical quantities have the same value.

Euler brick   A three-dimensional box on which the edges and the diagonals of the six rectangular faces all have integer lengths.

exegetics   A branch of algebra concerned with the manipulation of the symbols in an equation or proportion in order to determine the value of the unknown quantity.

exponent   A number indicating how many repeated factors of the quantity occur. Also known as POWER.

extrema   The smallest or largest values of a function corresponding to the highest or lowest points on its curve.

factor   An integer that divides a given integer without leaving a remainder.

Fermat prime   A prime number of the form $2^{2^n} + 1$ for some positive integer n.

Fermat's last theorem   A famous result in number theory stating that there are no positive integers x, y, and z that satisfy the equation $x^n + y^n = z^n$ for any integer $n > 3$.

fluxion   Sir Isaac Newton's name for the derivative.

fraction   See RATIONAL NUMBER.

friendly numbers   A pair of integers, such as 220 and 284, each one equal to the sum of the other's factors. Also known as AMICABLE NUMBERS.

fundamental theorem of calculus   The link between the two main ideas of calculus expressing the inverse relationship between the operations of differentiation and integration.

generalized binomial coefficient   An integer or fractional value given by the computation
$$\binom{n}{k} = \frac{n(n-1)(n-2)\cdots(n-k+1)}{k(k-1)(k-2)\cdots1}$$, where k is an integer and n is an integer or fractional value. When n is a positive integer, this computation agrees with the binomial coefficient.

geometric series   An infinite sum of the form
$$a + ar + ar^2 + ar^3 + \cdots$$

geometry   The mathematical study of shapes, forms, their transformations, and the spaces that contain them.

graph theory   The branch of mathematics in which relationships between objects are represented by a collection of vertices and edges.

gravitation   The attractive force that pulls objects toward each other.

heptagon   A polygon with seven sides.

hexagon   A polygon with six sides.

Hindu-Arabic numbering system   The base-10 place-value system of counting using the numerals 0, 1, 2, 3, 4, 5, 6, 7, 8, and 9 that was developed by Hindu mathematicians in India and Islamic mathematicians in the Arabic countries.

homogeneity   The property that is satisfied when all terms in an equation or polynomial have the same degree.

hydrostatics   The study of the properties of fluids.

hyperbola   The intersection of a cone with a plane that intersects both nappes of the cone. Equivalently, the set of points whose distances from two fixed points, called the foci of the hyperbola, have a constant difference.

imaginary number   A number that can be written as the sum of a real number and the square root of a negative real number.

inscribed polygon   A polygon whose vertices are all on the circumference of a circle.

integer   A whole number, such as -4, -1, 0, 2, or 5.

integral   A function formed as the limit of a sum of terms defined by another function. One of two fundamental ideas of calculus that can be used to find the area under a curve.

integration   The process of determining the integral of a function.

intersect   To cross or meet.

inverse-square law   The principle that the force of gravitational attraction between two bodies is inversely proportional to the distance between the two bodies.

irrational number   A real number such as $\sqrt{2}$ or π that cannot be expressed as a ratio of two integers.

iterative algorithm   A multistep method for solving a problem in which the approximate solution obtained in one step is used to generate a better approximation in the next step.

locus   A collection of points whose coordinates satisfy a given equation.

logarithm   A number indicating the exponent to which a fixed base must be raised to produce a given quantity.

logistic analysis   See ANALYTIC ART.

mathematical induction   A method of proving that a statement is true for all positive integers by first proving that the statement is true for the integer 1 and then proving that if the statement is true for some integer, it is true for the next larger integer.

maximum   The largest value of a function or the highest point on its graph.

mechanics   The branch of physics dealing with the laws of motion.

Mersenne prime   A prime number of the form $2^n - 1$ for some positive integer n.

minimum   The smallest value of a function or the lowest point on its graph.

minute   A unit of angle measure equal to 1/60th of a degree.

mystic hexagram   For any set of six points on a conic section, the 60 hexagons formed by these points and the 60 corresponding lines associated with the intersection of their opposite sides.

natural logarithm   A logarithm that expresses a given quantity as a power of the naturally occurring constant e, whose value is approximately 2.71828.

natural philosophy   The branch of philosophy concerned with investigating the laws of nature that explain physical phenomena, including physics, chemistry, mechanics, dynamics, optics, and astronomy.

negative number   Any number whose value is less than zero.

number theory   The mathematical study of the properties of positive integers.

optics   The branch of the physical sciences dealing with properties of light and vision.

orbit   The path of one heavenly body around another, such as the Moon's orbit around the Earth or the Earth's orbit around the Sun.

parabola   The intersection of a cone with a plane that intersects one nappe of the cone but not in a closed curve. Equivalently, the set of points equidistant from a fixed point, called the focus of the parabola, and from a fixed line, called the directrix of the parabola.

Pascal's triangle Rows of positive integers arranged in a triangular format in which the first and last entry in each row are 1, and each entry is the sum of the two entries above it.

pentagon A polygon with five sides.

perfect number A positive integer such as 6, 28, 496, and 8128 that is equal to the sum of its factors.

perfect square See SQUARE NUMBER.

perimeter The sum of the lengths of the sides of a polygon.

perpendicular Meeting at right angles.

philosophy The study of the meaning of life.

pi (π) The ratio of the circumference of a circle to its diameter, approximately 3.14159.

polygon A planar region bounded by segments. The segments bounding the polygon are its sides, and their endpoints are its vertices.

polyhedron A solid bounded by polygons. The polygons bounding the polyhedron are its faces; the sides of the polygons are its edges; the vertices of the polygons are its vertices.

polynomial An algebraic expression that is the sum of the products of numbers and variables.

poristics A branch of algebra concerned with the manipulation of symbols performed in the process of proving or illustrating a theorem.

positive number Any number whose value is less than zero.

postulate See AXIOM.

power See EXPONENT.

power series A representation of a function as an infinite sum of terms in which each term includes a power of the variable.

prime number An integer greater than 1 that cannot be divided by any positive integer other than itself and 1. The first few prime numbers are 2, 3, 5, 7, 11, 13, 17, etc.

prism A piece of glass in the shape of a polyhedron usually having a pair of triangular faces.

probability theory The branch of mathematics concerned with the systematic determination of numerical values to indicate the likelihood of the occurrence of events.

projective geometry A type of geometry concerned with relationships between points and lines in a plane to which an extra point has been added at infinity.

promptuary A 17th-century calculating device that performed multiplication by turning a set of metal plates arranged in a box.

proof The logical reasoning that establishes the validity of a theorem from axioms and previously proved results.

proper divisor For any positive integer, those smaller positive numbers that divide it.

proportion An equality of ratios of the form $a/b = c/d$.

prosthaphaeresis A method of computation that used relations between trigonometric functions to multiply two numbers by adding two related values.

pyramid A polyhedron formed by connecting a point, called the apex, to a polygonal base by triangular faces.

Pythagorean theorem The rule about right triangles that states: if a, b, and c are the lengths of the three sides of a triangle, then the triangle is a right triangle if and only if $a^2 + b^2 = c^2$.

quadratic equation An equation of the form $ax^2 + bx + c = 0$.

quadratic formula The formula that gives the 0, 1, or 2 solutions to a quadratic equation as

$$x = \frac{-b \pm \sqrt{b^2 - 4ac}}{2a}.$$

radius (1) The distance from the center of a circle to any point on its circumference. (2) A line segment of this length with one endpoint at the center of a circle and the other endpoint located on its circumference.

ratio The fraction obtained by dividing one number by another.

rational number A number that can be expressed as a ratio of two integers. Also known as a FRACTION.

real number One of the set of numbers that includes zero, the positive and negative integers, the rationals, and the irrationals.

reflection The behavior of a light wave as it bounces off a mirror or other surface.

refraction The bending of a light wave as it passes through a lens.

regular polygon   A two-dimensional polygon such as an equilateral triangle or a square in which all sides are congruent to one another and all angles are congruent to one another.

regular polyhedron   See REGULAR SOLID.

regular solid   A three-dimensional polyhedron in which all faces are congruent regular polygons and all vertices have the same degree. Pythagoras proved that there were only five such objects: tetrahedron, cube, octahedron, dodecahedron, icosahedron. Also known as REGULAR POLYHEDRA.

right angle   An angle with a measure of 90°.

right triangle   A triangle with one right angle.

root   (1) A solution to an equation. (2) A number that when repeatedly multiplied produces a given numerical value.

roulette   See CYCLOID.

ruler-and-compass construction   A plane geometrical diagram that can be created with the use of a ruler or straight edge to draw line segments and a compass to replicate distances and draw circular arcs.

second   A unit of angle measure equal to 1/60th of a minute.

semicircle   Half of a circle.

sexagesimal   Base-60.

sexagesimal fraction   A fraction whose denominator is a power of 60.

sextant   A mechanical device used to measure the angle between two distinct objects; used mainly in navigation to determine longitude.

simultaneous equations   Two or more equations relating the same variables that are to be solved at the same time. Also known as a SYSTEM OF EQUATIONS.

sine   For an acute angle in a right triangle, the ratio of the opposite side to the hypotenuse.

slide rule   A mechanical calculating device consisting of one or more logarithmic scales.

sphere   The set of all points in three-dimensional space at a given distance, called the radius, from a fixed point, called the center.

spiral   A planar curve traced out by a point rotating about a fixed point while simultaneously moving away from the fixed point.

square   (1) A four-sided polygon with all sides congruent to one another and all angles congruent to one another. (2) To multiply a quantity times itself; raise to the second power.

square number   A positive integer that can be written as n^2 for some integer n. Also known as a PERFECT SQUARE.

system of equations   See SIMULTANEOUS EQUATIONS.

tangent   For an acute angle in a right triangle, the ratio of the opposite side to the adjacent side.

theorem   A mathematical property or rule.

triangle   A polygon with three vertices and three edges.

triangular number   A positive integer that can be written as $1 + 2 + 3 + \cdots + n$ for some integer n.

trigonometric functions   The functions $\sin(x)$, $\cos(x)$, and $\tan(x)$ that form the basis of the study of trigonometry.

trigonometry   The study of right triangles and the relationships among the measurements of their angles and sides.

trisect   To cut into three equal pieces, as a line segment, a geometric figure, or an angle.

vacuum   A space containing no matter.

variable   A letter used to represent an unknown or unspecified quantity.

versed sine   For angle θ, the versed sine is $1 - \cos(\theta)$.

vertex   The endpoint of a segment in a geometric figure.

vowel-and-consonant system   The convention of using vowels to represent variables, and consonants to represent coefficients, in algebraic equations.

witch of Agnesi   The curve studied by Maria Agnesi corresponding to the equation $y = \dfrac{a^3}{x^2 + a^2}$.

zetetics   A branch of algebra concerned with the process of transforming a problem into an equation or proportion relating the known and unknown quantities.

FURTHER READING

Books

Anderson, Marlow, Victor Katz, and Robin Wilson, eds. *Sherlock Holmes in Babylon and Other Tales of Mathematical History.* Washington, D.C.: Mathematical Association of America, 2004. Collection of 44 articles on the history of mathematics through the 18th century.

Ashurst, F. Gareth. *Founders of Modern Mathematics.* London: Muller, 1982. Biographies of prominent mathematicians.

Bell, Eric T. *Men of Mathematics.* New York: Simon and Schuster, 1965. The classic history of European mathematics from 1600 to 1900, organized around the lives of 30 influential mathematicians.

Boyer, Carl, and Uta Merzbach. *A History of Mathematics.* 2nd ed. New York: Wiley, 1991. A history of mathematics organized by eras from prehistoric times through the mid-20th century; for more advanced audiences.

Eves, Howard. *Great Moments in Mathematics (Before 1650).* Washington, D.C.: Mathematical Association of America, 1983. Presentation of 20 major mathematical discoveries that occurred before 1650 and the mathematicians involved.

———. *Great Moments in Mathematics (After 1650).* Washington, D.C.: Mathematical Association of America, 1981. Presentation of major mathematical discoveries that occurred after 1650 and the mathematicians involved.

Gillispie, Charles C., ed. *Dictionary of Scientific Biography.* 18 vols. New York: Scribner, 1970–1980. Multivolume encyclopedia presenting biographies of thousands of mathematicians and scientists; for adult audiences.

Grinstein, Louise S., and Paul J. Campbell, eds. *Women of Mathematics: A Biobibliographic Sourcebook.* New York: Greenwood Press, 1987. Biographical profiles of 43 women, each with an extensive list of references.

Henderson, Harry. *Modern Mathematicians.* New York: Facts On File, 1996. Profiles of 13 mathematicians from the 19th and 20th centuries.

James, Ioan M. *Remarkable Mathematicians: From Euler to von Neumann.* Cambridge: Cambridge University Press, 2002. Profiles of 60 mathematicians from the 18th, 19th, and 20th centuries.

Katz, Victor J. *A History of Mathematics: An Introduction.* 2nd ed. Reading, Mass.: Addison-Wesley Longmann, 1998. College textbook; explains accessible portions of mathematical works and provides brief biographical sketches.

Morrow, Charlene, and Teri Perl, eds. *Notable Women in Mathematics: A Biographical Dictionary.* Westport, Conn.: Greenwood Press, 1998. Short biographies of 59 women mathematicians, including many 20th-century figures.

Muir, Jane. *Of Men and Numbers: The Story of the Great Mathematicians.* New York: Dover, 1996. Short profiles of mathematicians.

Newman, James R., ed. *The World of Mathematics.* 4 vols. New York: Simon and Schuster, 1956. Collection of essays about topics in mathematics, including the history of mathematics.

Osen, Lynn M. *Women in Mathematics.* Cambridge, Mass.: MIT Press, 1974. Biographies of eight women mathematicians through the early 20th century.

Perl, Teri. *Math Equals: Biographies of Women Mathematicians and Related Activities.* Menlo Park, Calif.: Addison-Wesley, 1978. Biographies of 10 women mathematicians through the early 20th century, each accompanied by exercises related to their work.

Reimer, Luetta, and Wilbert Reimer. *Mathematicians Are People, Too: Stories from the Lives of Great Mathematicians.* Parsippany, N.J.: Seymour, 1990. Collection of stories about 15 mathematicians with historical facts and fictionalized dialogue; intended for elementary school students.

————. *Mathematicians Are People, Too: Stories from the Lives of Great Mathematicians.* Vol. 2. Parsippany, N.J.: Seymour, 1995.

Collection of stories about 15 more mathematicians with historical facts and fictionalized dialogue; intended for elementary school students.

Struik, D. J. *A Source Book in Mathematics, 1200–1800.* Cambridge, Mass.: Harvard University Press, 1969. Excerpts with commentary from 75 influential mathematical manuscripts of the period.

Tabak, John. *The History of Mathematics.* 5 vols. New York: Facts On File, 2004. Important events and prominent individuals in the development of the major branches of mathematics; for grades 6 and up.

Tanton, James. *Encyclopedia of Mathematics.* New York: Facts On File, 2005. Articles and essays about events, ideas, and people in mathematics; for grades 9 and up.

Turnbull, Herbert W. *The Great Mathematicians.* New York: New York University Press, 1961. Profiles of six mathematicians, with more detail than most sources.

Young, Robyn V., ed. *Notable Mathematicians: From Ancient Times to the Present.* Detroit, Mich.: Gale, 1998. Short profiles of mathematicians.

Internet Resources

"Biographies of Women Mathematicians," Agnes Scott College. Available online. URL: http://www.agnesscott.edu/lriddle/women/women.htm. Accessed March 4, 2005. Biographies of more than 100 women mathematicians prepared by students at Agnes Scott College, Decatur, Georgia.

"Eric Weisstein's World of Scientific Biography," Scienceworld. Available online. URL: http://scienceworld.wolfram.com/biography. Accessed February 12, 2005. Brief profiles of more than 250 mathematicians and hundreds of other scientists. Link to related site Mathworld, an interactive mathematics encyclopedia providing access to numerous articles about historical topics and extensive discussions of mathematical terms and ideas, by Eric Weisstein of Wolfram Research.

"History of Mathematics," Simon Fraser University. Available online. URL: http//www.math.sfu.ca/histmath. Accessed January

19, 2005. Short profiles of a dozen mathematicians, from Simon Fraser University, Burnaby, British Columbia, Canada.

"Images of Mathematicians on Postage Stamps." Available online. URL: http://jeff560.tripod.com. Accessed March 6, 2005. Images of hundreds of mathematicians and mathematical topics on international stamps, with link to web ring of mathematical stamp collecting, by high school math teacher Jeff Miller.

"MacTutor History of Mathematics Archive," University of Saint Andrews. Available online. URL: http://www-groups.dcs.st-andrews.ac.uk/~history. Accessed March 5, 2005. Searchable index of mathematical history and biographies of 2,000 mathematicians, from the University of Saint Andrews, Scotland.

"Math Archives," University of Tennessee. Available online. URL: http://archives.math.utk.edu/topics/history.html. Accessed December 10, 2004. Ideas for teaching mathematics and links to Web sites about the history of mathematics and other mathematical topics, by the University of Tennessee, Knoxville.

"Mathematicians of the African Diaspora," National Association of Mathematics. Available online. URL: http://www.math.buffalo.edu/mad. Accessed March 1, 2005. Includes profiles of 250 black mathematicians and historical information about mathematics in ancient Africa.

"Math Forum," Drexel University. Available online. URL: http://www.mathforum.org. Accessed March 3, 2005. Site for mathematics and mathematics education; includes "Problem of the Week," "Ask Dr. Math," and *Historia-Matematica* discussion group, by School of Education at Drexel University, Philadelphia, Pennsylvania.

"Mathographies," Bellevue Community College. Available online. URL: http://scidiv.bcc.ctc.edu/Math/MathFolks.html. Accessed March 4, 2005. Brief biographies of 25 mathematicians prepared by faculty members at Bellevue Community College, Bellevue, Washington.

"Wikipedia: The Free Encyclopedia: Mathematics." Available online. URL: http://en.wikipedia.org/wiki/Mathematics. Accessed August 22, 2005. Online biographies with many links to in-depth explanations of related mathematical topics.

ASSOCIATIONS

Association for Women in Mathematics (www.awm-math.org) 4114 Computer and Space Sciences Building, University of Maryland, College Park, MD 20742-2461. Telephone: 301-405-7892. Professional society for female mathematics professors; Web site includes link to biographies of women in mathematics.

Mathematical Association of America (www.maa.org) 1529 18th Street NW, Washington, DC 20036. Telephone: 202-387-5200. Professional society for college mathematics professors; Web site includes link to the association's History of Mathematics Special Interest Group.

National Association of Mathematicians (www.math.buffalo.edu/mad/NAM) Department of Mathematics, 244 Mathematics Building, University at Buffalo, Buffalo, NY 14260-2900. Professional society focusing on needs of underrepresented American minorities in mathematics.

National Council of Teachers of Mathematics (www.nctm.org) 1906 Association Drive, Reston, VA 20191-1502. Telephone: 703-620-9840. Professional society for mathematics teachers.

Index